I0407465

Death

IS

Serious

By

Tombstone Todd

The

Undertaker

To the best of my ability this is how I remember the nefarious events of my life. This does not, in any way, mean that these facts are accurate. They are what I remember them to be. In other words, an attempt at accuracy was made, but don't bet your life on it.

Death is serious is not a simple dignified, economical look into the funeral industry. It is a slap in the face look with a bloody towel. Death is Serious presents itself like a virus in black and white, through a collection of stories told as if you were listening to them in a bar. In graphic detail, events which occurred behind and in front of that big green door are expressed that will captivate the curious, constipate the courageous, and instigate conversation.

Death is Serious may cause serious emotional outbursts. The reader accepts all responsibility for reading Death is Serious. Death is Serious will inform and prepare the reader for what's to come.

People die and you are there.

DEATH IS SERIOUS.

With Respect,

Tombstone Todd

The Undertaker

Tablet of Tall Tales

Morality is Life in Full Bloom

Fortune From Chinese Fortune Cookie

From the Beginning

"We have a call! You'll have to go on a call." The secretary was shouting at me, coming down the stairs out of the stately-looking building with its three matching sets of French doors in the front, and a heated portage along the side for the pallbearers' car, the coach, and a limousine. It was a very nice funeral home. The portage was a convenient feature which kept many toes from being cold during the winter, and it kept the people dry.

She said this to me and went back inside, as if this was nothing extraordinary.

Here I was: 18 years old, raking leaves in the front yard of a funeral home, and after being on the job for about 2 hours, I was expected to go pick up a dead body.

I washed the dirt off my hands and stood around waiting, not knowing what the hell else to do or what I was up against. I didn't really think about it too much. I didn't have time. I was a kid who needed a job and had found one as a groundskeeper at a funeral home. About 15 minutes later a black Mercury station wagon with frosted windows pulled up into the circle drive. My partner was a little older, had on a nice black suit and had long black hair.

We pulled out of the driveway and down the street and ended up in some neighborhood not far away. It was in the fall, and the mid-morning sun made the leaves shine. I had my window down, my arm outside, resting on the edge. I was told to roll the window up; it doesn't look good. As we turned a corner and entered the street where the house was, we saw several police cars and lots of people standing around and milling about. It didn't really hit me until we pulled up in front of the house that they were all waiting for us. TAA DA!

We parked in front of the house and got out. My partner went up to a cop, who had started to walk our way. I stood beside the station wagon and watched the crowd watching me. My partner and the cop talked a little and motioned for me to walk with them up the driveway into a single garage, tucked under the house.

Inside the garage there was a beat up, tan, mid-70s Chevy 2-door Malibu. The small garage had wheels and tires leaning against the walls, and shelves full of oil cans. There was very little room to move about. In the car, in the driver's seat, sat a big man - a REALLY BIG dead man. He was wearing shorts and a T-shirt. The floor of the car was covered in beer bottles. His head was bent down and his chin just about touched his neck. Should I mention, at this time, the smell inside the garage? No, I'll wait. He was purple from the chest up.

Well, after my partner looked the scene over we went back to the station wagon and he opened up the back door. The whole neighborhood was still watching us. Inside was a cot, and he reached in and pulled it out. It had collapsible wheels, which dropped to the ground as the cot left the car. As I didn't know what to do, I just stood there, trying to look cool, calm, and collected, in my T shirt and jeans.

I bet we made a striking pair. We rolled the cot up to the garage but there wasn't enough room to bring it inside, so we parked it near the end of the car. There were a bunch of cops, standing outside and a coroner standing inside. The cops were talking and writing up their reports, and probably laughing at us behind our backs. This was one body they were glad not to move.

My partner unzipped the black canvas which covered the cot. This revealed a smooth, soft mattress inside. It was red. There was a white sheet, folded neatly, and a pillow as well. He took the sheet and told me what we were to do next. We were to unfold the sheet and place it over him, with most of it on the right side. Then, together we would roll him towards us and tuck the sheet under his butt and back, and pull it out from the left side. "Ok?" he asked. "Sure," I replied.

Sounds easy? Well…have I mentioned the smell yet? Yes, well, the smell was twice as strong reaching inside the car to lay the sheet over him. That smell was coming from him. And there I was leaning over his body with a sheet in my hands actually touching him. He was cold, kind of wet or maybe moist would be a better word, and soft, yet full, like a sponge full of water.

When we had the sheet over the body it leeched to him like water to cotton. Oh, shit! It did smell! Nobody told me that this guy had been dead in his car for four days. I noticed that his neck and face were blue, but at that time I didn't know that this was a sign that he had gassed himself to death.

There was an 8-track player under the steering wheel with a tape in it. I wish I could remember what tape he had playing. It was a son-of-a-bitch to get his right leg around it, the leg was stiff, yet pliable, and his calf was stretched tight like a balloon.

Fluid in a body will always settle into the lowest parts of the body after death. You can blame that on gravity. Well, it wasn't a second after we rolled him toward us, when all this blood, slime, and ooze, came pouring out from the skin on his thighs and calves, which had split open. We had just unstuck him from his beloved car seat. While most of the skin stayed on the seat, the fluid splattered everywhere. It covered the seat, dripped down onto the carpet, and ran all over my hands and arms. The smell and the sight of this made the cops leave the garage faster than a "free donuts" sign at Dunkin' Donuts. Slime and ooze was everywhere. And it was on me.

No, neither of us was wearing gloves, aprons, or masks.

Imagine what it would be like trying to slide and lift a 250-pound pile of semi-soft, yet stiff, oozing human flesh in the form of a body, from around a steering wheel of a 2-door car with an 8-track player blocking the way of the right leg under the steering wheel. And do it in a garage so narrow that the car door wouldn't open all the way. Well, it was an experience that changed my life.

Once we had the wet sheet wrapped around him it was time to slide him out of the car, then up and out onto the cot. Behind the cot stood the cops and behind them stood the rest of the neighborhood. Everyone was waiting for us.

I started gagging and it took a while for me to stop so we walked outside to breathe in some fresh air. We went back in.

As the space was limited, it was very hard to get a good hold of him inside the sheet, and keep our balance. Slowly we slid his big wet dead ass to the edge of the seat and up into our arms. He and I were now touching chest to chest with my one arm under his hip my other arm around his neck. His was a face only a mother could love, I will never forget. We placed him down on the trunk of his Chevy and then slid him off it, picked him up again and walked out into the mid-afternoon sun into the eyes of the all-seeing public. We placed him onto the red mattress where we seat-belted and zipped him into the black canvas pouch. He was not going to get away. Then, as respectfully as two kids could, both soaked from head to knees in who-knows-what, we walked the cot down and placed our prize inside the back of the Mercury. I'm sure we left a trail.

The rest was easy. We got in and drove back to the funeral home. The whole process hadn't taken more than 45 minutes. On the way back we wiped ourselves off with some towels. The driver dropped me off and took the body to the other funeral home the company owned. I went in and washed myself. The little lady who lived upstairs gave me one of her dead husband's shirts and a pair of pants to wear and I went back outside to finish raking leaves.

The boss arrived back from lunch, and after hearing about the call, walked up to me and said he was amazed I was still on the job. A month later, he took me to a whore house and we shared a nice lady friend of his.

That was my first day on the job. I can still remember the dead man's name. Kind of like the first girl, you never forget their name.

And on the Seventh Day

I went on a few more calls while I worked at that funeral home. However, at my first job in the funeral industry, which lasted about a year, I learned how to wax wood floors, clean toilets, vacuum carpets, wash cars, rake leaves, and clean windows and chandeliers with vinegar. I was hooked.

I had now graduated from junior college with a bullshit degree and had been accepted in a "prestigious" private Catholic college in a big city on the coast. I had learned how to study, smoke pot, and party like there's no tomorrow. This school accepted those who had the time to fill in all the forms to get all the grants and student loans or those who had the money. I didn't have any money, but I filled out the forms and was accepted. Now I had to move and find a job.

The very first day after class there was a keg of beer and a party going on for the students on the school grounds. The school even had its own bar, open only on Fridays. I liked this place.

This school was full of students with money. Quite of few of them were foreigners from oil countries. They drove Firebirds, Datsun 260Z's, or black Pontiac Trans Am's, like in the movie "Smokey and the Bandit. They wore all the latest designer clothes. All the girls who liked money would go after these guys. I watched how some of these girls manipulated these rich dumb bastards and got them to buy them expensive clothes. They had everything going for them. Except that this was during the time of the Iran Hostage Affair, and to us, Iranian or Saudi Arabian, they all looked alike... There were the occasional car fires and consistent verbal barrages and rallies.

During my college days, I was into drinking, smoking pot, staying in shape and trying to screw all the girls I could. This was and still is the first and most important part of college life, I think. Studying comes second.

I had only one problem: I didn't have any money. So I needed a job.

I was living in the big city with a good friend, who was also attending the same private college. He and I had been selling our plasma to get some money and I was getting tired of that. It was in the early eighties. Have you ever sold your plasma? It's a great idea that is quite an experience and has come a long way since 1980. You are lying on a bed in a room full of, what appears to be bums and drunks, while they take out what seems like a gallon of blood from your left arm. Then, after centrifuging out all the good stuff from your left arm, they put the leftovers back into your right arm. The cold remnants of what's left. Burrrr! I felt that stuff going in me all the way up to my shoulder. The whole process took 2 hours or so, and I made 15 dollars. I decided there had to be an easier way to get some money

One day I opened the phone book and wrote down a few addresses of funeral homes. I owned one suit at the time. My father had bought it for me after launching my career in the funeral business. It wasn't really a suit, but a blue nylon sports jacket and polyester gray pants. I had a white shirt, a gray tie and black plastic shoes to match. I put it on, hopped into my 1973 Pontiac Catalina and drove to several funeral homes to try my luck. I also had prepared a very simple resume, complete with mortuary experience and a college degree. I visited several funeral homes that day, left my resume at each, and talked to a couple of owners and managers.

I didn't get any jobs right off in the funeral industry. It might have been due to the fact that I had hair down over my ears, but I don't know for sure.

I did, however, through the school, get hired part-time at a fire station as a hose-coupler man. The station I worked at was more of a warehouse than a fire station. Next door was a fully-functioning fire station. Where I was, we had hoses and clamps and numerous boxes of fire equipment. We were the supply center. The basement was full of antique fire equipment. There were several wood fire call boxes, with glass doors; the type that used to be mounted on street poles. There were fire bells, and old fire hydrants that probably a hundred long dead dogs had pissed on. I used to like to go down there. I wonder if that equipment is still there.

My job was to make sure the hoses in the warehouse would all hook together. You don't want to show up at a fire and not be able to reach the fire because the hoses don't fit together. At least, I think that was my job. All I did really was ride around in a red pickup truck and deliver toilet paper and paper towels to the numerous fire stations in the city. All the hoses had already been checked. We were also delivering notices with new rules and regulations about equal rights to be put up on the wall of all the fire stations.

This was in the early 80's, and women were now becoming firewomen. I never went to any fires. I worked there a short time. I was back in the funeral business when the first women fire fighter, I believe, in the country was killed responding to a fire alarm called in from a private college within the city. She was riding on the back of the fire truck, and fell off. It was a false alarm. I think it originated in a dormitory, pulled by some idiot. She lost her life for nothing. That was sad.

On the Job as Herman Munster

One day, during the start of summer break, I got a call from a funeral home I had left a resume with. It seemed that a gentleman they had working for them had suffered a heart attack and would not be able to return for work for quite a while. Would I mind coming in for an interview?

Back then, when I thought of funeral directors, the only kind that came to mind was old, tall skinny, slow-talking, long-limbed, quiet types. Those were the only boys I had worked for. My opinions of undertakers came from my previous year in the business and from television. Undertakers were personified as being strange, with odd behaviors or odd, with strange behaviors. And those were the good ones; the bad ones might be the type to laugh and kick an injured puppy, and smile as it died.

You really believe you can judge the person by the looks? Read up on some undertakers sometime.

How do undertakers get that way? How does anybody get that way? God only knows. When the common denominator is death in all its glory, it seems to prove limiting to find any type of balance or normalcy in social conduct when you come at it from those extremes.

Blowing Smoke at the Interview

I showed up for my interview on time and in my one and only suit. These funeral directors were a little different. Most of the guys were young. I mean, I was 21 and they were in their 30's and 40's. A few were older, but everybody had a joviality about them that seemed to me pretty laid-back. The place was really busy and the guys were coming and going all the time. They were joking about their day and everybody was really friendly to me. The personality of the whole place was right.

The interview went very well. The boss smoked cigarettes right on through to the end.

They called me up the next day. When could I start?

I went to work in my plastic shoes and cheap suit the next Monday. I had the usual forms to complete that accompany any new job; like a W-9, and the employment application. So I started filling out the forms. The first form I filled out was an application to join the A Union. This funeral home was different. This funeral home was a union shop. Most of the funeral homes in the city were union.

Yep, I was now a card-carrying union man. In my opinion, unions are great. They may be the best thing for employees and the worst for employers. I don't know. I was an employee. I appreciated being a member for 10 years and they did right by me. I'm vested and if I reach the not too soon age of 65, I'll get a retirement pension from them. That is, unfortunately, a hell of a lot better than most employees gets from their employers. It costs around 30 bucks each month for your membership, plus 100 bucks to join. No problem. I would earn that in a week. I was on summer break from school and I was working full time!

As a union man, we were paid a very good wage, had good benefits and for working overtime we were paid at time-and-a-half. WOW! At my first job, and at almost all the others after, you worked for your monthly salary. And you had better be happy with *that*! Which meant that just because it was Christmas and you were with your family, when the phone rang you had to go to work; or when it was 4am, and you hadn't been home since 8am yesterday, that didn't matter, you made the same!

On the flip side, in small funeral homes, sometimes, you wouldn't work at all the whole month. You waited, and waited for the phone to ring and relieve you from being bored to death. This was worse, because you still couldn't go anyplace, you was on call. There was a time I worked at a very slow funeral home and I would not get a call for several months. Even though I never lifted a finger, you might say, for two months, I was still chained to the place. I spent my time waiting by drinking, toking, riding my Harley, and learning to play the guitar.

There is an old mortician's motto, you will find in a trade magazine or on the front of a baseball cap:

"When your day ends, mine begins"

It makes sense.

I wrote a song "Tombstone Todd the Undertaker," which has the line:

I'm Tombstone Todd the Undertaker,
Well, at least that's what I'd done,
When your day's over, don't you worry,
My day's just begun.

Making Bread on the Dead

Being paid for working overtime in a funeral home is a beautiful thing.

I started working the next week and was making more money per hour than I could hardly spend. The overtime was great, and we were paid every Friday. When I started, we figured out our own paychecks. We handed in the slip, and received a check.

Just about everybody in the place worked 20 hours of overtime a week. Death is a 24 hours, seven days a week business, and I was cashing in on it.

We were a busy funeral home. And a damn good one too! It seemed as though I had fallen into the busiest funeral home in the state, loved by all the families they had served (and still do I hope).

We were hated by almost all the other funeral home owners for doing the same as them for so much less than them. We were taking away their bread and butter.

We were the contract holders for the first memorial society in the country. Many hundreds have started up since then, but this was the first; simple, dignified and economical. Those were the words we lived by. When it came to funerals or cremations we were by far the cheapest and one of the best. Memorial societies provided a less expensive way of burial or cremation to folks and this one was really taking off. I was starting my second year as an appreciative funeral director and embalmer, and that was how I was reared within the industry.

Give them the best for less, and they will love you to death.

We would get phone calls from funeral homes in other cities and towns to come and pick up so-and-so, because the family had found out that the dead person belonged to the memorial society we contracted with. Most funeral homes wouldn't match our charges, so they would have to call us. They had wanted to charge the family 3 times what we were charging, but the family wasn't buying. Some of these funeral homes really hated giving up their dead to us. Some firms would make us wait for an hour to pick up the body, and then not help us move it from their table to our cot.

Shit You Oughtta, Gotta Know

I was shown a trick on how to move a body from a tray onto a cot on your own. You need to know this kind of information when you are alone, and it's time to move old Joe from the morgue tray to the cot. Ask as politely as you may, and as often as you want, but old Joe still ain't going to help you. The move is easy, quick and simple really. All you do is lift up both legs, together, high enough to get the butt up and out of the tray, and quickly flick the butt over the end of the tray, and it will land on the cot, bringing the head and arms with it. The cot must be in the right position: not too far away from the tray, nor too close. If you put the cot in either one of these positions, you will land the body half way on the cot, and soon it will be down on the floor. If you really screw up, the cot will fall over too. If you really fuck up, the body and the cot will fall on you. I know it's happened to me.

We had so many bodies we hit the streets running.

I was driving all over the state picking up dead bodies and bringing them back. Most of our families wanted cremation services so when I would get back to the funeral home all I had to do was identify the body, place it in the refrigerator made for 20 bodies, and go home. We used two old walk-in refrigerators made for ten each but we economized and doubled up on the shelves. We also used two rolling racks which each held several more bodies.

To Be or Not To Be

You do not have to be embalmed if you want to be cremated. You may not have to be embalmed if you want to be buried, but, if you want other services, you may have to be embalmed.

Say, you want to be cremated, but first, your whole family and a bunch of friends wants to come take a peek at you, to mourn and cry, or sing and dance over seeing you dead. That type of visitation is usually done without embalming. That is sort of an in-and-out type of visitation. If however, you are about to start gurgling from the nose and mouth and mess up our viewing table because your family really doesn't like you, and they take three weeks getting around to finding the time to drive the, say, three blocks to the funeral home, to take a three minute look, you are going to have to be embalmed, like it or not. No funeral home will keep you, lying around taking up space, for show and tell, for that length of time. They might let you have a week, if they have a refrigerator. But it's going to cost someone.

If you want be become a crispy critter, and you don't want anybody to see you and if nobody wants to see you either, you do not have to be embalmed before we hit the gas.

But, if you want to have your body sent to Katmandu, Nepal, or Death Valley and buried there, well... plan to lie around a bit while we will fill you up and send you on your way.

If you plan to go to Hell when you're dead, go. As for me, I've been to Hel Poland, and it's a lovely little seaside village on the very end of a narrow spit of land. I've also been to a temple of sorts about Hell, along the Yangtze River, but that's another story.

Let's say you want to be buried. And you don't want to be embalmed. In the twenty-first century it's sometimes called a green burial. Do you have to be embalmed? Well, in the twentieth century we called it a direct burial, but to answer the question; it depends on you and the pre-arrangement you made with a licensed and respectable funeral director. If you have all your ducks in a row, t's crossed and i's dotted, if you have done all the leg work possible when you still could walk and if you have down on paper that you don't want a funeral, don't want embalming or a viewing…. Well, maybe, and I say maybe, you won't be embalmed. This of course still depends on several things; namely, your family and Johnny Law.

After you drop dead, your family can change your decisions. Believe me, this happens more than you might think.

Let's say the above scenario is true. We have you lying in a casket, dressed, unembalmed, and are waiting patiently for the cemetery to finish opening up the grave. The pre-paid, signed, no- embalming-requested contracts in hand. But, right in the middle of loading you in the car to take your last road trip, we get a phone call from your long-lost daughter. "You can't bury her without allowing me come to say goodbye. I'll be there in three days."

If that happens, out of the casket you will come, and you will be undressed and embalmed and then replaced in your new digs. This is so you won't look like a three-day-old dead, unembalmed body when your daughter shows up, but you will look like you just passed away in your sleep. Your appearance, looking nice for your daughter, is better business for us. Don't swell 'em; don't tell 'em, just sell 'em. Now, that makes sense.

This might be the philosophy some used car dealers believe when they shine up an old wreck.

The embalming was maybe done just because of appearance, at no cost, but not always, and sometimes ahead of consent. Remember this was 1980. Cell phones and computers weren't common. Once someone left for the plane, train, car or bus, they were outta communicado with us.

We are stuck in the middle.

What the hell do we, the undertakers, do? If we don't embalm your ass, and bury you, as you requested and don't let the daughter see you, she will sue us and soon she will be the new owner of a funeral home.

If we keep you around, down in the fridge, don't embalm you for three days, let your daughter, her new boyfriend, their children and whomever, see you decomposing right before their eyes, we are screwed again! We're probably get sued by your daughter, and/or you might haunt us for years!

OK, let's change the setting a bit. Say, you are so afraid of fire; you can't even light a match. The last thing in the world you want to have happen to your holiest body is for it to go up in a puff of smoke.

You want to be embalmed, put on display with all the bells and whistles, viewed by any and all, and have a chapel full of teary-eyed friends at your funeral, and then buried in a fine casket wearing your Sunday best, next to mama. But now, in walks your son, the eldest son, the executor of your estate, and a pain in your ass since birth, and to save money, he requests or commands us to cremate you.

Now what?

We can't do both.

When this happened to me, I called up the person, who is the relative next in line, and/or the next person in charge of dear old Dad and explained the dilemma to them. I then let them call up this long lost son, and explain the facts of your life and death to them.

More times than not, the daughter or son wins out in the end and you get the opposite of what you wanted. He gets to take a peek, and then you go in the ground. Or, you get the gas, and he gets the cash. We hope you are an understanding and friendly ghost. And, since you're of no help in your defense, we usually have to do what we are told to do, by people who can speak. It's the law, and with the law, death is a different matter altogether.

It's the Law

The law can make us hold your body, unembalmed, and lying on a refrigerator shelf, slowing rotting away for weeks. If they, the law, or us, don't know who you are, you ain't going anywhere fast. The law can have you autopsied with a stroke of a pen, if they think some hanky-panky was going on, and your death was mysterious. It don't matter much what arrangements you have made for yourself, if your death involves the law somehow, the law and us will be looking at your body very closely.

Many times a person had said to me, I don't want anybody coming and looking at me when I'm dead. If they can't come and see me when I am still alive, to hell with them. Many times, however, I have let someone see them.

Women are funny about being seen dead; more so than men. Maybe they are still worried about their weight; who knows.

A good funeral home plans for the unexpected. By this I mean everybody that leaves the place dead should look like they are alive and well, and could go shopping. This happens to us all the time. Someone, usually a distant family member, will want to see the body. "Please, just a quick peek, after the funeral, and before you leave for the cemetery". They might want to place in the casket a note or a flower or whatever. Some just want to know that you are really dead and not out there on the lam, getting ready to spend the life insurance. If the funeral home pops open the lid of the casket, and didn't dress her, close her mouth and eyes, and make her look nice, they're in deep shit. I have never had this happen to me, luckily. I always tried to have them looking good. The times I didn't, I got away with it.

We had a specially built refrigerator that would hold 60 bodies or more. There were shelves six high all along the sides and we had movable racks as well. The bodies were placed on white plastic-covered sheets of plywood. To get the bodies on and off the shelves we used a hand powered, movable hoist. The refrigerator was intimidating to the Joe average undertakers who would stop by from time to time. Nobody ever ran as many bodies through a funeral home as we did. We were the Costco of funeral homes. Seldom were we ever busy enough to have 80 bodies on ice at one time, but it happened. In one 24-hour period we brought in 23 bodies. I remember one month we brought in almost 250. That's a lot of bodies, and most undertakers working in the area were amazed. They would handle 20 or 30 a month, and be busier than a three-legged Billy goat during mating season.

In the early eighties we had two walk-in coolers to store the bodies in. It was packed two to a board most of the time.

A couple of times, when we would have 5 funerals to deal with in a day and we were short-staffed, I would mix up the flowers and set the wrong ones up for a service. Everything would go along fine, until the service ended. Then, as the family came up and inspected the flowers to see who sent what, they would come to me and say, we don't know this person. Or, they would say to me, this card says the flowers are for Mr. Jones' funeral, this is Mr. Smith's funeral. Hell, I screwed up the flowers so many times, I could tell by the puzzled looks on the faces of the families when I had done it again. When it happened, I would run to the flower room and try to sort out whose flowers were whose, and what flowers had gone where. If Mr. Jones' flowers were already in a hearse, heading for Mr. Smith's funeral, I was fucked. This happened to me several times. It really pissed off the families, and I understood why. Some people would go ballistic; others would be more understanding. Because of my fuck-ups, I have had to call up local flower shops and have them make up and deliver special flower arrangements. Pronto!

I had a great flower shop I used, which was operated by some Chinese. They helped me many times in my frequent times of trouble. They liked me and would give me from time to time a dozen roses. This was another big bonus to being an undertaker - the flowers. I used to recommend that flower shop to families who would call in or ask if I knew a good flower shop. They did a nice job.

As the saying goes: "You rub my back and I'll rub yours."

Flower Power

I have had little old ladies complain about the size of the flower arrangement, the color of the flowers, and how they were arranged in the pot. Funeral flowers are the oldest flowers in the flower shop. They're only meant to last a short while, and then it really doesn't matter after the funeral what happens to them. Sometimes we received flowers that looked worse than the dead guy. I'm talking about wilted and wrinkled old flowers. These really bad arrangements I would send back. I learned a little trick to make flowers last a little longer. You pour in a little Seven-up. That makes them spring to life again, if you can say that about dead flowers.

When I was a kid we used to throw out the flower sprays after the services were done. The plants and many of the arrangements are given to the family or sent to various places, as the family requests, i.e. hospitals, nursing homes and churches. After throwing away what seemed to be several dozen roses and carnations and the like over several weeks, I said bullshit to this! My girlfriends were always living in flowers. Yea Haw! Well, as you know all good things got to come to an end, and it was the same with the flowers. The boss caught me, so I stopped. I stopped being so obvious.

Some of the flowers I would receive for a service were covered with pollen. When I would have to move them, say, from the visitation room to the chapel, or worse, from the car to the church, my suit or shirt would get covered with white or yellow pollen. This was annoying, and you learned to watch out for those types of flowers. When it happened to me at a funeral, I would walk around with a yellow and black suit for the remainder of the service, and still try to look professional.

Dead Reckoning

We used to identify bodies in the old days using a good old marking pen. Write their names right on their legs. No toe tags or wrist bracelets to fall off and get lost. That system worked very well, because it was simple and direct. Now days they use wrist bracelets and toe tags, to properly identify a dead body in the funeral home so that Mrs. Jones really is Mrs. Jones. There have been over the years several mistakes made with this method. I have read about them happening in hospitals and at funeral homes. It's a real boo boo, when you open up the casket, at the end of a perfect service for the final walk by, and inside is Barney Rubble instead of Fred Flintstone. I still prefer writing right on their leg.

The Basement

The basement of my funeral home looked like it was right out of a Vincent Price movie. You could film a Dracula movie without changing anything.

The basement was lit by 2 light bulbs when I started. Each one was hanging from the end of a cord, at each end of the basement, which was about 3 cars lengths long and about two cars wide. It had big columns along one side to support the upper 3 floors. Gray concrete was the color of choice in those days.

For the first few months, at night, if those two light bulbs weren't on, when I drove into the basement after picking up a dead body, and turned off the car headlights, it would be blacker than a coal digger's ass in there. There was always in the background the hum from the crematories, and I was so sure the bodies and the monsters were going to get me that I would leave the headlights on until I could get to the light switch.

There were 3 crematories in the basement. These were kept going 24 hours a day. My and everybody else's job was to do everything and anything to keep the place running efficiently, and correctly. And so we did.

And God Created Woman

We all got along together very well. This wasn't so tough when you consider we were spending almost more time at work than at home. Not the best solution for the guys with families, which everybody had but me. I wanted to work, I liked the money, and I also enjoyed their company. Because we made such a good team we never really had personnel troubles. At least until we hired our first woman undertaker…

She came, and we abused the hell out of her, and she was gone soon. She stayed 3 or 4 months. I think we just about gave the boss a heart attack from stress just worrying when the phone call would come in saying something about a sexual harassment lawsuit. I feel bad about that now, and think that women play a vital role in the industry. But, back then, Shit, a woman! This was a man's job.

We weren't supposed to swear in front of her or make crude, lewd and rude gestures. I just didn't think I could adjust. And when she left, we were back to an all-boys club.

That was the only time I have worked with a woman undertaker. I am an old dog, but if the opportunity ever came up, I could be taught some new tricks, and I would work alongside them nice and pretty.

I have worked with the boss' wives, and that has to be worse. Some of them think they know more than their husbands. Through osmosis, they know more about embalming, making funeral arrangements and funerals than you do. They, one must remember, are married to THE undertaker. Some have good ideas. Some don't have a clue. One thing, for sure, they certainly know more than you. They married the owner, and you didn't.

Dreaming Big

Once, a guy at the funeral home came up with the idea of all of us buying a big yacht. We would take turns yachting around the lakes if you will. We all would share all the costs and we would rent it out to help make it pay for itself.

Man! I was all for the idea. I was 23 or 24, had the money for my share, and could just imagine 4 or 5 lovely ladies, lying topless, maybe even bottomless on my private yacht somewhere under the sun, enjoying a three hour cruise. Beautiful! I'd buy me a captain's hat, and I'd be skipper of the U.S.S. Getting Laid.

By the middle of the first week he had found one, and we had all been down to where the boat was moored.

Boy, it was a beauty! A 1940's Chris Craft. Around 48 feet long, flying bridge, twin Chryslers, 3 staterooms, two bathrooms, WOW!

It was all restored and it was so big, it needed about 3 guys as crew just to get it out of its slip and under way. By the end of that first week, we were all hot and bothered and ready to sign the papers. The weekend came and went, and on Monday, well, the wives had put the boot to that idea. Damn.

Working on the Chain Gang

Working in a funeral home that handled over 2300 bodies a year is an undertaking. Someone had to load and unload the crematories three times a day and conduct 3 to 5 funerals a day, just about 7 days a week. Plus, we had 2 hearses, 2 call cars, and one errand car on the road just about every day, and they had to be kept clean. After I had been there a week or so, they sent me on my first of many journeys up to a hospital about 4 hours away to bring back the dead. Alone.

We had always gone in two's to pick up the dead. We went to hospitals, nursing homes, houses, trailers, apartments, and all-too-frequent accident scenes. If, another man was needed to lend a hand, and help lift and move the body, he was there. Nowadays there is more help at these places and the undertaker goes alone. It also costs less money.

When I look at myself in the mirror and think about the sorry fellow who, if alone, will come to pick up my fat ass, I wonder... If he doesn't have help, he will wrench his back and be sore for the rest of his life. Do the words, State Industrial, ring a bell?

Well, I jumped in the classic black Mercury station wagon, with the traditional „S" bars on the side and the silver tinted windows. It had the big fancy decal of some Egyptian urn on the back window too. It was air conditioned and it had a stereo. I took off. Hell bent for fury, out of town.

People look at you funny when you drive one of these cars.

I pulled up at a McDonalds drive through and ordered two cheeseburgers for me, and one for the guy in the back, just to get the reaction. When they were handed to me, I would throw one in the back just for kicks. This would usually freak out the window tellers. I used to love to do that.

When you drive a funeral car, unusually fast and furious, people get out of your way. Maybe, thinking, that death is just passing them by this time. They don't like looking out their rear view mirror seeing that death is on their bumper, catching up to them, or just following right along.

I was flying up the road because, didn't ya know? Now, I'm on a mission from God. When the person in the car in front of me would look in his or her rear-view mirror, see me, in my black hot-rod Lincoln, Mercury funeral car, they would jump in their seat, pull over and let me by.

I LIKED THAT! I was the fastest guy on the road.

I have gotten out of many speeding tickets over the years, being an undertaker, driving funeral cars and my own cars. But I wasn't impervious; I've had well over 40. When I was pulled over, I would tell the officer, that I worked with the force as an assistant coroner and a mortician. It worked many times, and it has saved me a hell of a lot of money in fines, and insurance. I still like to drive fast.

Meeting the Owners

I met the owners of the funeral home I now worked for on one of these missions. They were retired folks, a very nice people. His father had started the business during the start of the 20th century, which seems like ages ago. He had believed in the simple philosophy about giving the public good service at a reasonable rate. This worked and he and the other funeral home owners in the area made a good living. Fifty years ago, along comes a memorial society, and he gets the contract to deal with all their dead. I don't think the other funeral home owners wanted it. Fifty years later, when I met him, he was laughing all the way to the bank.

His father had two sons in those days. Together they operated the funeral home
This was good for me, because they were into motorcycles; specifically, Indian and Harley Davidson motorcycles.

When I started there, Indian and Harley Davidson parts were tucked all over the place in the basement. These parts had been there from the 40's and 50's. Gas tanks, fenders, tools, just lots of stuff. No one had touched them, and they were there. Right up until sometime after I left to go to mortuary school in the mid-1980.

You see, I just had to make a real, down to earth, licensed, undertaker out of myself.

During my absence they hired another apprentice who either threw them out, God forbid, or sold them. I think the latter happened, as he wasn't into motorcycles at the time.

Shit!

Years later I found a wrench with the Indian trademark on it. It said Indian motorcycle.

That was all there was left of the tanks, fenders and chrome bits that used to litter the place. They needed the space.

The Fat, Fatter and Fattest

Also during my absence, this funeral home had the distinct honor of bringing in an 800 plus pound dead man. It seemed this fellow had got sick in his home, and had to go to the hospital. He weighed a hell of a lot more then. When the fire department and the ambulance came they had to remove a window to get him out and into an ambulance to take him to the hospital. There, he lost quite a bit of weight, but didn't like the food, and died. The funeral home had to bring the hospital bed with him in it, back to the last-stop shop. They had to use a winch to get him out the bed, and into a specially built casket. I would have liked to have been there to see him. I think he is listed in an old copy of the Guinness Book of Records.

We are a country with a lot of fat people. To all those fat people out there, watch out, the undertakers of your city are watching you, hoping they won't be on call when you die.

Remember; you can drink the ugly pretty but you can't drink the fat thin.

Hey, There's Someone Dead at Your Back Door

In all my years, I have had only about 4 families bring their dead to me. I thought that was pretty cool.

One man brought his business partner in the back of a homemade traveling wagon. It was a truck that was all painted up like it was used in a carnival. It had a bed and came complete with a working pipe organ.

Another brought her husband to us in the passenger side of the Cadillac he loved so well. I asked her if she had received any funny looks, and she said "No, I put a pillow against the window so it looked like he was sleeping." And in she drove.

I don't remember how she said she got him into the car.

At one funeral I was conducting, I talked to a man who told me about his grandmother's funeral. He said they buried her, behind the wheel, in a very nice old car, inside a hill on some property they owned. Using a front-end loader, they dug out the side of a hill big enough for the car. Put her inside, behind the drivers' wheel, and pushed it in the grave they had created. Then they covered her up. He said that when his grandfather died, they were going to dig the car out again, and put him in the passenger side. That sounded cool to me, I thought, but what a waste of a classic old car. Doesn't matter, he said, they had two. I wish I could remember what kind of a car it was. I would like to be there when they dig that car back out, because it would be interesting to see how it stood the test of time. I also would like to see the faces of the folks when they see granny's face.

Phone Etiquette

When people call you by the hundreds over the years and tell you they have had a death, and they want you to come and pick up their father, mother, sister brother, aunt, uncle, friend or foe, you obtain the innate ability, just by listening to their voice over the phone, to pretty well know what to expect. Some folks were in shock, others were pissed off, and some couldn't care less. I became good at predicting.

One lady called up and said. "There's a dead body and it is, DEAD ON THE FLOOR!" She yelled this about 5 times into the phone.

This helped me immediately understand the situation she was in. Well, not really. "THERE IS A BODY, DEAD ON THE FLOOR?!!" I asked, "Where are you at" and she said, "in my living room and there is a BODY, DEAD ON THE FLOOR!"

I finally got her to provide me her address and a partner and I went to the house. Sure enough, there was a dead body lying on the floor in her kitchen. Turns out, it was her husband, and she was, of course, in shock. We took care of the situation by removing the dead body lying on the floor.

She kept on saying, all the while we were there, that she had just come home from the store, and there was a BODY DEAD ON The. FLOOR... Over and over, and over and over...

Why is Mom So ... Cold?

Did you know that a dead body, immediately after it dies, warms up a little? Know why? Well, it's very scientific, and very complex, but I can explain it to you in a minute or two.

The main way a living, breathing, human body eliminates heat is through breathing and sweating. The skin releases sweat, and up through the skin on your head heat will escape.

Remember your momma saying to you as a kid to wear your hat?

The heat that occurs right after death comes from all the little cells in your body, still having a good time, multiplying. When you fall over dead, those poor little cells are having so much fun; they don't know you're dead and they party on! And that generates the heat, which causes the temporary increase of the temperature of the dead body. It only lasts a little while and then goes away. I never witnessed it occurring; I guess I wasn't fast enough at getting there.

I have had several people ask me why their momma was so cold. I tell them the same story about the cells, and, that in the end the body is the same temperature as in the building.

Maybe the casket companies should put electric bed warmers inside the caskets. We could crank up the heat, and you'd be toasty warm to the touch. You'd be a Dead Hot Toddy!

As for Rigor Mortis, well, we all know him. He allows us to be able to pick up little old dead men and women, and not have their arms and legs swinging in the breeze, as we carry them to the cot.

When we doll you up, drop you into a box, and put you out for show, did you ever notice that the hands are crossed over each other? It sure looks comfy doesn't it?

It is.

I have been in the undertaking business so long I can't get to sleep unless I lie on my back with my hands crossed. It actually isn't too uncomfortable. Try it.

Other times, we are covering up an I.V line that had left a bad bruise of the back of one hand.

Did you know that Tod in German means death? That was confirmed just about every time I introduced myself riding my motorcycle around Germany. I don't think my parents knew that the name they bestowed upon me at birth would be the Alpha and Omega of my existence

Trying Hard Not to Put Your Foot in My Mouth

They make you take psychology classes in mortuary school so you can become an expert on figuring out what people feel when someone they love dies.

Yea, right. I say, "Bull shit!" No one knows what it feels like when somebody else's mother, father, sister or child dies. NO ONE. Except that person.

I've put my foot in my mouth a few times learning that lesson.

One time while I was making funeral arrangements, I asked a woman what her mother had done as an occupation for the majority of her life.

It's a question for the death certificate, I explained. And it is. She replied her mother was a housewife. I asked: "Just a housewife?"

JESUS CHRIST! You should have heard her yelling. You could have if you were within a two-block area. "Just a housewife, why you pip squeak, She raised 5 kids, kept a clean house, clothed and fed the whole family while my father was working hard to provide for us, as best he could. She would sew our clothes well after everyone had gone to bed so we would look nice," and on and on she went. She even stood up for a while. Well... you get the picture. I sat behind my very important desk and wished I could have crawled under it. I had meant the question in a different way, but it came out wrong.

I have to type the occupation of every dead person who I have dealt with on their death certificate. And some people think I have a strange job.

If you were under-water deep sea biologist, specializing in the chemical alterations of the DNA of 612 species of fish, living deeper than 300 fathoms under the sea, for 3 months of your life, and a tree trimmer for 20 years, what was your usual occupation? You are a tree trimmer. But, whatever you tell me, I'll type it on the death certificate.

No, I have never ever listed: bum, or jack-of-all-trades and a son of a bitch. Although many families have said that's what they did and were.

Making funeral arrangements consists of listening, writing, and doing. The family comes in, tells you what they want, you tell them what you need, and you write it down, and do it. It would seem to me, that anyone with the intelligence to hold a pencil could do it. So why have I made so many fucking mistakes writing stuff down? I wish I could tell ya. Maybe, my fingers move faster than my brain or the opposite. It could have been the whiskey, might have been the gin, and could have been the three or four six packs. I don't know.

One of the most important details that the undertaker needs to take care of, when making funeral arrangements, is getting the information correct for the death certificate and getting the death certificate typed correctly. Back in the 1980's the death certificate was a carbon-copied form. Every mistake was double. White out worked, sometimes, but if there was a major mistake, the certificate would come out looking like an infant typed it.

The death certificate requires about 25 questions to be typed on it correctly; 18 questions to be asked of the family, and roughly the same amount concerning how the death occurred, with the answers to be typed in correctly. This means spelled right. The right date of birth, place of birth, full name, parent's names, including the mother's maiden name. It took me sometimes 2 or 3 times to type all the information, correct, onto a death certificate, without fucking something up. My fingers would sometimes hit the wrong key, just to piss me off. Or, I would be typing something on the wrong line. This usually happened to me right near the bottom of the certificate too.

I learned early on to type in the death certificate completely, and correctly, before you send it off to the doctor's office for their signature. It looks real bad when you have to go back to the doctor's office to bring back a THIRD copy of the death certificate, because you fucked up the first two he had already signed.

Furthermore it really looks like you are a dumb ass, when you hand the wife or the daughter a certified copy of the death certificate of her husband or father, and they come back to you and say you have misspelled his name. I have done that a time or twenty. I try to check and recheck so that doesn't happen and it doesn't happen that often, but when it does, boy do I look like the dumb ass.
When you have to have to change a death certificate, it can go fast, if you know the folks over at the courthouse and they like you.

It pays to be on the good side of the people working in the Register's Office. I have made sure over the years to take them flowers and chocolates. Most funeral homes bring them gifts on Christmas. One time, on a really hot day, I brought in a box of ice cream bars. They have caught my mistakes and corrected them without even telling me before they make up the certified copies. The copies aren't cheap. Thank you to all who have saved my ass, and reputation.

You need a correct death certificate to get your hands on the money the dead person might have. You also have to be legally entitled to it. The death certificate, with your name typed in as the legal informant is the key to the cash machine. I have had some people get really pissed off because I have accidentally mistyped something on death certificate, which then had to be redone. This has put a roadblock between them and their money and they were not happy.

If it has been a while, say, 4 or 5 days or a week or two, after the death certificate has been filed with the county, and there was a mistake, it could take a long time to get the change made. The death certificate must go to the state's head office for recording. After it leaves the county court house, it's out of their hands and into the hands of the bureaucratic machine. It can take a month or longer to get a corrected copy of the certified copy of the death certificate back and into the wet and greasy palms of the family that can't wait to spend the money. I would bet some people had already spent what they didn't have and needed it to cover their debts.

Know a Seamstress Who Can Mend Straight?

Doctors have to list the cause of death on the death certificate. Some go into great detail, listing all the causes in the world which might have killed this dead guy. Other doctors, I have seen are more to the point. They simply write down, Alcoholism, AIDS, and smoking.

But does anybody really know what, exactly, we die from, when we die?

An autopsy is the only sure-fire way I've been told to determine the exact cause of death.

If you ever get the chance to see an autopsy done, go see one. Most times, tickets are hard to get. They slice and open you up, and you look like one of those little boxes of cereal you get at a restaurant. The smell is a wonderful aroma, and might make a nice perfume for pathologists looking to meet other pathologists. Then they open the head.

It's amazing to watch how the skin of someone can be pulled, with the hair on it, back to front and down over the eyes; simply amazing. The skull is cut, using an electric saw with a round blade, in a circle above the ears. The pathologist will leave a notch in the temporal bone, a.k.a. the forehead and the skullcap, to help hold the two pieces back in place. The skin will fold back over the skullcap and nicely into place when he's finished.

Brains weigh a lot, and they go plop when you drop them on the prep room floor. I've seen brains, and I've seen brains, and I've seen people eat brains and eggs.

In the old days doctors used to do a hell of a lot more autopsies on dead people to find out what killed them. Some would do a terrible job, and cut up the arteries that I need to use to embalm, making them almost unusable.

That makes it tough. I hate embalming an autopsied body. It takes 2 to 3 hours, sometimes, and, even a nice one is a hell of a job. If you have to dig around for a half hour, to find and pull out a very fragile carotid artery that was cut so short by a doctor, that has, for all practical reasons, sucked itself way back up the neck to use to embalm the head with, it makes the job, OH! so much more fun. It becomes more interesting when the pressure (and sometimes the volume) is too high on the embalming machine and you swell a head up. More specifically, an eye looks like a golf ball, or the neck looks like an inner-tube. Good God! I've done that a time or two, too.

If you like to sew, you can come work for me. It takes a long time, after you have already spent a long time finding the right vessel and shooting the magical juice down each leg, down each arm, and into the head, and trunk, to sew a body back together. And I mean by sewing you pull back together the 50 pounds of fat each side weighs like a rag doll. Some folks weigh less, others weigh much more. However before I sew you up, I have to deal with the guts, and the brain, and then put them back into place, all properly embalmed. Guts weigh a lot too. If you don't double up on your Hefty bags, watch out. Guts on the floor make a big fucking mess. Yummy!

Hefty bags. Yep. We used 'em. There are lots of brands of plastic bags out there. When you are autopsied the doctor usually will cut out certain organs and take a close look-see. (I've seen a lot of strange things…More to come.)

Then, after the pathologist is satisfied, those organs and all the rest of your guts go into a (hopefully) strong plastic bag. Then we sterilize the guts, tie up the bag good and tight, making sure we get all that delicious air out the bag, stick it back in your belly and pull you back together using some strong-ass thread.

Sometimes you come out looking like you lost weight.

Now, let's sew up your head!

The incision goes from ear to ear. Making sure the skull cap is secured onto the base of the skull is very important. You can't get it backwards, thank God. Making sure the inside of the scalp is dry is good, as is making sure it's dry inside the skull. But, making sure you don't get hair in your stitches is a Bitch. Of all the stitching an embalmer has to do, stitching up the head is the most time-consuming. It takes quite a while to move each hair out of your way as you go along. The stitching has to be as tight as a baseball. I'm usually humming a country song. When it's all said and done, and the body is on display, and there isn't a wet stain on the pillow, you've done a good job.

Most times there is a stain and if the family can see it you better be Johnny-come-quick, with another pillow and a sheet so they don't see it. However, many do, and many have sued.

We can put Humpty Dumpty back together again, but it's going to take time, a whole lot of precious time. Not your time. My time.

It used to be that the cost of autopsying a body was paid for by the hospital, if the person died there and there was a question. It still is, if that happens. Now days, the percentage of autopsies are way down, and the cost of having one done, is way up there.

Does it really matter how, exactly, dear old granny died, after living to the ripe old age of 98? If so, call us up, and we will get her autopsied for ya. Expect to spend a grand or more - plus our additional charges.

Used Parts

I had a family one time request an autopsy for dear old dad. He had died just after having come out from being under the knife. I was standing there, watching the autopsy and watched the pathologist remove a small cotton pad that was left in his chest. "Umm," he said, "that's not good. That didn't kill him though"' he said quickly to me. Um. Hm...

Many, many times I have swept out the crematory and found a set of forceps, or other tools of the surgical trade laying there among the bones. Were these left in during an autopsy or during surgery? Were they left in this dude? Did they kill this man? To find out the answers to these questions, find this guy when you die, and ask him.

When you do a lot of cremations you're left with a lot of spare parts. We had a garbage can we would fill up with hip replacements, splints, braces, all with screws to match. An Erector Set of sorts. Back then, when it was full, we would throw it in with the garbage in a sturdy plastic bag.

I had a couple of glass eyes, but that's in a different part of these recollections.

We had lots of prosthetic legs and arms and would sometimes put them under a car, or put one hanging out of a door and bring the office girls down to scare them.

Boiled Potatoes

Have you ever peeled the skin from a boiled potato? I just did for the first time in my life, a week ago.

I cook to eat only.

It immediately reminded me of the skin of a very old person. Very thin, and easily torn. More than once, I have been washing the body of a dear old dead lady, after a perfect embalming, and have not been gentle enough washing her hands. The skin on the back of a hand would peel off. If you notice it quickly enough, you can gently put it back into place, and it will re-attach itself. A small amount of make-up and no one will notice. If however, you are in a hurry, and don't notice it until the skin is dry; you have just made yourself a lot more work. You can hope that it was the right hand, as we usually place left over right when it comes time to laying you out. We reserve the right, however, to make changes when necessary.

If you smoke that yellow stain on your fingers won't wash off. God knows I've tried.

To Shave or Not to Shave

Have you ever shaved anybody else? I have shaved more people than most. Women and men. Shaving a dead person is a fine, skillful and gentle art. An art that demands a slow, gentle hand and a good, sharp razor. Any good undertaker knows that.

Many years ago, for a funeral conference at some out-of-the-way place, I brought a body over to be embalmed. An embalming company had a new kind of embalming fluid they wanted to sell us. They needed a body to embalm, to prove how great this new juice was. I was told to bring old Joe Blow, a good old boy from the fridge. I put him on a cot, loaded it in the back, jumped in the car and drove over. When I got to the hospital where the convention was being held, I unloaded the body onto a table and went to be with the others.

There were several of us undertaker types sitting in this auditorium, in the basement of a hospital just waiting to be amazed by this new, wonderful type of embalming elixir. It was a type that didn't need mixing with water, as all the others did. This was just pure sweet concentrated 100% juice.

The head salesman, an embalmer himself, rolled out the body and started shaving him. After about 20 minutes or so, a kid from the audience yells out, and it wasn't me, some rude remark about taking longer to shave than to embalm. Well, the old boy explained that the face is looked at the most, and therefore demands the most attention to detail, hence a slow careful shave. He was right. The guy I had brought over did have a 4-day growth as I remember. The shaving and embalming went fine.

I don't know of anybody that uses the waterless, 100% percent pure, all natural, chemically enhanced embalming juice. I don't think I know many who ever did.

What choice do you make when you receive a lovely old lady who has, for whatever reason, unfortunately not been able to address her own facial hair? Maybe you shave, maybe you don't.

The rule was to always shave. It goes back to first impressions make better business.

However, you probably will get in a pickle if you shave off Gramma's moustache. The moustache that she proudly wore for the last ten of her ninety-eight years.

Now you've stepped in shit.

Same goes for men. Say, the guy liked to wear a 4-day-old beard. He liked the old rough-and-ready look. He has looked this way for thirty years, and now here I go and shave it off. This IS the way he likes to look. If I shave him, I might just change the very awareness of his soul. He might end up, because of me, somewhere between Yin and Yang.

Sure, you might look better, but you DON'T look like you.

What do you do then? I had an old undertaker tell me that you need to use pubic hairs to replace facial hairs.

I've been lucky. I've never had to use the tweezers for that.

If you are careful, you will shave a dead man perfectly. If you hurry and nick him a bunch you will leave him with enough razor burns that his face will look like 9 hole golf course.

Don't do this. If you do, time to yell, MAKE-UP!!

It's better to trim a beard or mustache before you shave it off. You can always re-shave 'em. I didn't like the idea of using tweezers…

Mingling with the Boys

Funeral Industry conventions are a funny thing. They are held once a year, in the usual public convention centers with big hotels. They are held in the bigger cities throughout the country. What's funny is that they can be going right alongside say, the National Used Car Salesman Convention. The mixing of us with you makes for funny conversations.

I have only been to two conventions. The first in the basement of an old hospital, next to the morgue. The second was a first class event. The bosses go to these.

It was held in a big hotel, in the middle of summer, next to a lake. The place was jammed with undertakers, their spouses, and me. I was looking for the free hand outs: great pocket shoe polishers, and checking out the new must-have funeral merchandise.

Huge rooms are filled with the latest caskets, music systems, books and folders, urns and cemetery equipment. All kinds of embalming fluids and new cosmetics were on display.

It is quite amazing how much stuff an undertaker needs to buy, and all you have to do is die.

What was really funny was listening to the non-undertaker guests, who were also staying in the hotel. They talked about us under their breaths, as they would wander by and gasp as they looked in at the caskets and urns on display.

I asked a lady in an elevator once what was going on, and she said: "It's a convention of *those guys*... You know, in *that* profession."

The hotel parking lot was awash with new $65,000 hearses and limos, vans and suburbans.

Some folks might be shocked to see 5 hearses in row parked beside the hotel they wanted to or were staying at. I saw some people turn about-face and walk around to a different entrance.

I had to stay for all the meetings and shows. They were interesting in a morbid sort of way, and I may have learned a thing or two. I enjoyed participating in the drinking sessions, which also ended each of the three days. That's where you learn all the gossip.

Ever Know a Killer?

It was a sure thing that this undertaker had a monkey on his back. He was a hard drinking, smoking man; very moody and dark. We had many drinks together over the years at district meetings. He ran a fancy funeral home, buried all the rich and fine folks. Turned out he killed his (ex) girlfriend the very week he was elected the youngest president of some fine civic organization. This was some 30 years ago. Only now, some 30 years later a police detective asks him for a mouth swab just to check some things out, and BOOM. The next day he shows up at the job, says a few things, and goes out by his truck and shoots himself in the head.

An undertaker friend of mine had a co-worker who made a cremation arrangement with an old fellow. He paid for everything and when it was all complete he also walked out the front door and shot himself on the front steps. This guy had his shit together.

I wonder if the undertaker had prepaid for his funeral.

Tit for a Tat

One time I said fuck in front of my boss's wife. She thought I said Fuck you, meaning her, But, I said, Fuck. I was looking at a death certificate.

We were busy as hell that day, and I was having a rough time. Two high school girls I had known for years had been killed. They were hit head on. I had worked on one of the girls and didn't even recognize her. I found out by reading about it in the paper. The next day, I was in the preparation room, working on another body, trying to get it embalmed, before I had to leave and make funeral arrangements with my friends. We had a funeral going on, and the phones were ringing off the hook. I was stressed out, and I asked the boss's wife to type up a death certificate for me to take. She was sitting at the only desk with a typewriter, bullshitting with another undertaker, who we did a lot of work for.

She had typed her husband's name in the box marked, funeral director. I asked her to change it, and, to please type in my name. She used white out, which looked terrible, and typed over my name on it. There was also a corrected spelling error about something else.

When I went in the office to leave, she said, "Here, hang this on your wall", and handed it to me. Well, "fuck" I said, under my breath, when I looked at it. It looked like a mess. She heard me. She went through the roof! She was screaming and yelling and I ignored all of it. She was yelling so loud you could hear it in the chapel. One of the guys walked back, saw her having a fit, closed the door and left. About then, the boss drives in, as I was leaving. I was so fucking mad, I just jumped in the car and left. I drove a block before I realized I had forgotten to take the cot, and the paperwork. I drove back in the garage. My boss was wondering what the hell was going on. I told him my side of what had happened and left.

I cried for the first time driving up to see my friends that day.

Over the next few days, it was cold as ice in that funeral home. My boss stood up for me, and I know that took guts. The next day, he came up to me as I was embalming a body and said, "I know my wife's a bitch. I live with her. But please don't tell her to fuck off again". I said "I won't".

To get back at any one she was mad at, it would seem that she let her fingers do the walking.

She would ring our pagers at the start of a funeral. Right when she knew we would be leading the casket, pallbearers and family quietly down the aisle in the church. Ring-ring went the phone or beep-beep went the pager. This looked really good! We learned to turn off the phones and pagers when we were working a service. Anytime an undertaker's pager goes off or his phone rings and people hear it, they all look at you and wonder who has died. You know that's what they're thinking.

Most times, they're right. Somebody has.

Did you know that some religions have a set way of bringing in a casket into the church for a funeral? In a Catholic service, the casket is to go into the church feet first. When the service is over, it is turned around and rolled out feet first.

Other churches want it brought in and out head first.

Some don't have any preference. The nice thing is that most people don't know the foot end from the head end of a casket, so if you fuck it up it, hopefully no one notices. Well, sometimes the preacher does, and sometimes someone in the audience does or your partner does. Look for the label, that's the foot end.

Cold Emotions

When you are an undertaker, you get to see, feel, hear and take from people, all kinds of emotions.

Once a man came in to make arrangements for his mother. After we finished he asked for the ring that she wore. I called upstairs to have someone retrieve it and tried to make small talk. That didn't go very well, as he was in a hurry and, well, couldn't we hurry things up a bit. 'Look" he said. 'You can cut off her finger, I just want that ring." Honest Injun! Well, I was shocked! I said: "We don't need to do that." So we waited. In the business, we'll use soap and a string. Soon enough he had his ring and I have this memory.

One of the best pieces of advice I ever heard, and never forgot, was that which came from a teacher at Mortuary College. He said when making arrangements with a family, never say, 'Well, God would have wanted it this way' or 'It was God's will'.

His point was, by saying that; I, the all-important undertaker, the one who comes during the night and whisks away the death, had maybe just talked to God on the phone and received his approval that it was OK for this person to die.

How the hell would anybody know what God's will was?

I have heard that same saying or a saying similar a hundred times from a person, undoubtedly trying to mean well; I can't count them all. It happens every day and I have never interrupted anyone for saying it.

It's interesting to listen to the things people have to say about each other when they hear about a death. Some mean well and others don't.

They come in and say' "That no good son of a bitch owes me $1000.00, and now, I have to pay for their God Damn funeral too." "Why, they haven't called me in 15 years. And the last time they did, it was to borrow money."

Nice people come in too.

Nine Lives

Some folks care more about their pet than parent or child.

People come in to see me and request that when they die, could I get someone to kill their dog or cat and have it buried with them? Or cremated with them? "Yes," I say, "we'll handle all the details"

I have buried and cremated maybe 4-5 dogs and/or cats that were, until a few days ago, alive and well, with their owners. Luckily for me the family had someone make the hit on the pet; I sure as hell wouldn't and couldn't, do it. They brought the pet to me in a sack. Sometimes I have had to use the humane society to cremate the pet. Sometimes, a veterinarian has to get involved to put the pet down.

I have to keep the now dead pet in the refrigerator until everything is ready. Then I'll place it in the casket nose to nose, if requested. One lady wanted to have her cat in the casket, with her during the funeral and I was to open the casket at the end so everybody could see. Her son nixed that idea, and I put the cat in at the cemetery, after everybody had left.

If the owner has chosen to be cremated, I again, have to get the pet killed, plus have it cremated. It's a no-no to cremate man and his best friend together....Tee hee...

I will intermingle the cremated remains of pet and owner; together for all eternity.

I've often wondered what the pet thinks of this idea.

You know it's true, well maybe it's true, but when the owner of a pet is laying dead, somewhere in the house, their pet acts differently. Have you ever witnessed that? I have.

Size Matters

I have poured the cremated remains of people into the most interesting of containers. I put a woman into a fruit jar, because she liked to make jam. Another time, a cook died and I put him into a pot and glued on the lid. A golfer went into a golf club; a biker went into a Harley gas tank. Two men were shot into space.

You can bring me anything that is hollow and I will put in it as much of you as I can. Just tell me what you want done with the rest of your ass. A golf club or fruit jar won't hold all of anybody.

This is why we, the problem solvers in the world of death, offer scattering services.

The first and most important thing to remember when you are going to scatter someone is to stand upwind. I have stood witness and watched a few folks stand downwind and get a real taste of old Joe. I was going to mention something, but the urn was opened and shook out before I was even close to the group.

We got a call one time to come and claim an urn from the sheriff's office. The urn had floated up on shore. Someone had found it and turned it over to the local police. They opened it up, found the ID disc, which had our name on it, and called us. We contacted the family, and they told us they had thrown it overboard, off a ferry. We took it back out to sea. We opened the container and correctly scattered the remains.

I once poured the owner of a restaurant all over the roof of his building. In time, he really did go through the roof.

Someone, (me) should parlay up the idea of mixing everybody's cremated remains together, add a dash of cement, a pinch of glue, bake at 400 degrees, for 3 hours and pour. Make sidewalks and roads. Okay, roads might be a stretch; how about pathways and trails…Might work.

Speaking of cement;

If you like the ocean, I hear you can have your cremains mixed with cement and placed in an under-water cemetery, complete with pillars and lions guarding the gate. Go to Cuba and turn north.

That's Pretty Cool.

Time Travels Back

People are into details when it comes to funerals. Some have been planning their funeral since birth, it seems. They must be related to the ancient Egyptians kings.

I checked out the Valley of the Kings outside of Luxor, Egypt. I had to see how the really old boys in the business did business.

The Egyptian kings and queens looked forward to death in a big way. Thousands would die building a tomb that would hold the body of the Pharaoh. The tombs actually hold the bodies of many servants who would be killed to help the dead king in the great beyond.

In Egypt, when I was visiting the Valley of the Kings and Queens, I bribed an Egyptian native standing inside one of the tombs, and he took me on a little side tour. With the help of his old, dim yellow flashlight, I saw a chamber where there were hundreds of skeletons. They were the servants who were killed to serve the king in the afterlife.

I have been twice around the world. I visited, because of what I did for a living, a lot of funeral homes and walked through many cemeteries on my travels. It's the same old thing, People live, people die, and somebody has to touch the dead. It's how they do it that's interesting. Remember, death is serious. No matter where you live.

You don't have to travel. You don't even have to go out your front door if you don't want to. Many people have never been anywhere, and they are just as happy as the guy who has been everywhere. I was told of a story while I was riding around the Isle of Man, that one little lady who lived there had never seen the sea. The whole Island is some 30 miles long and 4 miles wide!

Life happens every day you're alive, so enjoy being alive as you may.

Just don't let yourself be cheated out of doing something you have always wanted to do. Time and time again, I have had an old lady or man come in and tell me their story. "Well, we always wanted to go to Hawaii, but we just never got around to it. You know, kids and jobs and bills to pay". "Yes" I would nod my head. "And then, just when we had the time and money so we could go, George up and died," they would all say.

I live by a simple philosophy: Live.

Me and My Harley

Well, there I was, a highly paid funeral director and embalmer, living the high life in the big city, in high style, and traveling at warp speed. What's next? I bought a Harley.

I would ride my Harley to work when it was nice. I had to wear a suit every day and had to have short hair. I looked a bit un-Harley like to the unsuspecting. But that was okay. I got just as many looks from people for riding my Harley in a suit, as I did riding in my genuine horsehide leathers. After work I would ride to the bar, and have a drink or 10 with my friends. The bar was only a half a mile.

I was a greenhorn, just-bought-a-Harley, badass. So don't mess with me.

I had to work on Saturdays. My days off were Sunday and Monday. I hated that at first. I thought it meant that I would miss out on all the rides and the Saturday fun. And it did. Most rides started and concluded at the bar. The run would begin by leaving the bar Friday night after several drinks, and riding to some pre-determined site, set up a camp, and party all Friday night. Saturday night was also consumed by alcohol. On Sunday, everyone would ride back to the bar.

Quickly I found out that working on Saturdays wasn't so bad at all. I could still be at the bar on Friday night and be able to watch the boys leave. Saturday would come and go, and at 5:30PM I would pack up and ride off and make the party just when it was in full swing. Sunday would arrive and all of us hung over boys would ride back to the bar and drink some more. Luckily, I didn't have to work on Mondays.

I could sleep in.

I was making so much money that I could afford to fly all over the place. I went to Hawaii, California, Europe; and on around the world. I even bought a house.

One day it all came to an end. One day the little old lady who owned the place, came in and said: "Boys, I sold the place to a corporation, but don't worry about your jobs." She got 2 million bucks; all of us got the shaft. Well, they did re-hire back a couple of the guys. The new owners had to fire us all, because we were a union shop. That way they could break the contract with the union, and start again non-union. This was in the beginning days when big corporations were starting to buy up all the funeral homes.

They had a better idea. Their idea was to up-sell EVERYBODY who came through the door.

When we each went for the interview, everybody was nervous. I brought in a copy of all the funeral arrangements I had made that year and the stack of thank you letters from families I had quite a stack, and I still do.

I think I made a good impression on the big boys during the interview, and probably would have been rehired. But, I thought I was a big shit, and after the interview I went back into my office, put my feet up on my desk and played my guitar. The new boss walked by just then, and I don't think he liked that. I didn't get rehired.

Fifteen Minutes of Fame

The Union bought me a new set of tires for my car and a yo-yo. How many people can say that?
I spent 10 years in the union, and I walked a picket line with my fellow undertakers. I had only been with the

company one year, and the undertakers union went on strike.

The City was without people to pick up their dead! Well, not really. Our pop shop had this memorial contract that HAD to be maintained, so we were approved to keep working. We had to pay dues to help out the other boys, and picket during our off-time.

Picket!

Shit Man, I was 21 and picketing in a fancy suit, walking the sidewalks with the old boys in front of funeral homes while they had funerals going on. Unbelievable! This all started in the summer.

One day, because it was so damn hot, I rode to my assigned funeral home on my bike in shorts and a tank top. So I would be comfortable, I had a plastic recliner bungeed on back. I sat there for my 3-hour shift, drank lemonade, and got a suntan.

Another time, it was a holiday. I can't remember the year, but we were still on strike and I had to walk a picket line, alone in front of a funeral home. Because of the holiday, I wore a suit jacket. Most days I wore jeans or shorts.

Across from this funeral home was a convenience store so I wandered over for a cup of coffee and some beef jerky. I spied a yo-yo and bought it.

Back at the funeral home, I walked back and forth in front of the entrance with my picket sign.
It said UNFAIR such and such on one side and ON STRIKE on the other. I walked back and forth in front of this funeral home for 3 hours practicing my yo-yo technique. I have always liked yo-yos and was envious of people who could really make one do tricks. But I never did spend any time trying to perfect the damn thing.

Well, soon enough, after several cars had honked and people had waved as they drove by, a car stopped and a man got out. I didn't know who the hell he was.

He said he was from the paper and that the paper had received several calls about a good looking young man in a suit picketing in front a funeral home on this nice holiday and playing a yo-yo. Would I mind if he took my picture for the paper? Why not, I said. I remembered turning my sign around so that the best side showed and started to yo-yo.

Well I don't know much about yo-yo posturing or such, and it showed when I appeared big as life, on the front page of the morning paper.

Boy!! The phones did ring! I bet my picture is still on the wall of the funeral home where I was picketing.

The union enjoyed the publicity, and I was glad I had worn a suit that day. I sent a copy to my parents, saying look what your kid has done.

During the same time, while we were on strike, someone punctured all four tires on my car.

I remember walking out into my garage the morning, after making a late night death call. I got in the car, started it up, and put in reverse, and it didn't move. Ummm. I got out and noticed that all four tires were flat. The car clearly looked a bit lower than usual. I was in a hurry to get to another funeral home to picket, so I slowly drove the car across the street to a gas station, filled the tires with air and drove across town to another funeral home. I had time to tell my story to the boys before heading to a tire shop. I got all kinds of sympathy from my fellow picketers and the union paid to replace my tires. The union held a rallying party for us undertakers later that week. They presented me with a Light in the Dark, yellow yo-yo. I kept that yo-yo for a long time. We settled the strike, and went back to work. The Union was very, very good to me.

There supposedly was a rumor going around that my car was misidentified. My car and another undertaker's car, who works for us, looked similar. Same brand and similar color. That sort of thing. Well this fellow, it was rumored, was SCABBING! He was working for a different shop, under the table, and against the union. Well, some of the boys were looking to get even with him, and they went by our funeral home, saw my car and punctured the tires, thinking it was HIS car. OOPS. Oh well.

I don't know if that story is true, but if you read further, you will be able to decide for yourselves. This undertaker I mentioned I apprenticed under. He will prove to be to be a very interesting and most resourceful influence on me.

Bobby Pins

We use to have all kinds of strange people show up for funerals. We had one particular man who had for years, with his mother, attended funerals. His mother sadly died one year. Yet, as faithfully as before he would still show up. We called him Bobby Pins, as he had several bobby pins in his hair. Over the years I got to know Bobby Pins. I met him when I starting picketing.

He wouldn't come to just any funeral. He would show up when someone important died. Anytime a funeral home in the city had a funeral for some high and mighty person, you could bet money, Bobby pins would be there.

He smelled a little, and wore old dirty clothes but he was really a very kind man. He would always leave when asked. But you had to ask. If you didn't catch him at the door, and you let him in, he would walk up and down the aisle of the chapel taking pictures of everyone.

I don't think he ever had any film in his camera, but he liked to take pictures. He would walk right up to the front and take a picture of the casket, and the flowers. He would take as many pictures as he could, until he was asked to leave. We would escort him out the door and think we would be done with Bobby Pins. Nope! Sure enough, by the time we would arrive at the cemetery, there stood Bobby Pins.

He knew the bus routes! He would be standing at the front gates taking pictures of the procession.

I used to tell people who complained or asked about him, that it was an honor if he attended the funeral. It was, in a way. He only attended the best funerals. Bobby Pins was a true spirit. The movie "Harold and Maude" is a good sequel to the life of Bobby Pins. Rest in Peace.

This Old Man

Death is a 24-hour business. Very rarely while working in the big city did I get a complete uninterrupted night's sleep. This didn't bother me too much at the time. I was young, liked the money, and was staying up late anyway.

We had an old man working for us during the first three years I worked at this funeral home. He had been in W.W.II, and was in the Pacific Theater. He told me that the first Jap he killed was sitting over a fallen tree on some island taking a shit. Death didn't faze this guy at all. He liked it. Death meant money.

He also liked me. I think, because I lived close to the funeral home and could respond faster than anyone else, I was his apprentice.

He showed me his war scars once. His chest along the left side was all scarred up, where he was hit by machine gun fire.

He and his partner were in a foxhole, on some island in the Pacific and it was raining hard. They were taking a lot of fire from the enemy. Along comes a new recruit, fresh from boot camp and jumps in their hole. Shortly afterwards a grenade lands in there with them.

According to him, standard practice in such a case was to jump out, let it explode and then jump back in. That was a hell of a lot safer than looking for a live grenade in a wet, muddy hole, find it, and throw it back, within the allotted time.

Well, he and his buddy jumped out, but the third guy bent down to grab the grenade, and was blown to pieces. He took the dead guys dog tags, and later, while on his way to inform someone about what happened, he was shot full of holes. His dog tags were shot off, and when he woke up some time later in a hospital, he was listed as being the dead guy from the foxhole.

He, himself, was listed as lost in action. It took some convincing to get the whole ordeal straightened out, as to his real identity, and the identity of the Marine in the manhole.

He would carry a gun when we would go on late night calls. One of the other guys who worked with us told me a story about going on a call with him:

They were stopped at a red light in a bad part of town, the old guy in the passenger seat, young guy at the wheel waiting for it to turn green. A street bum came up to the driver's window and was demanding money. He started banging on the window. The old guy told the young guy to lean back in his seat. The old boy pulled his pistol out of his shoulder harness, leaned over, and put the muzzle of the gun against the driver's window, pointing straight at the bum's face. That scared the bum, and he left fast.

Together, this old man and I made lots of house calls together. We were meeting people who, in their time of grief, were greeted at their front door by a crotchety old man and a naive, young kid.

He didn't have much sympathy for the feelings of those who had just experienced a death. He would say things like, "Look, we will cremate the body, just sign here." Or, "Now pull yourselves together; I have to get these questions answered."

His mannerisms were a little shocking to me, but I was a kid, what the hell did I know?

I bought a Playboy magazine once and let him read it in the car one time while we went on a call. He liked that. I liked to hear him tell stories about the war.

He was as tight as bark on a tree when it came to buying anything.

One time he and I went to a house and picked up a dead old man. He had died just as he walked into his house and was lying on the living room floor.

The next day, I met the family and made the cremation arrangements with them. The man's wife asked me to return the new pants that her husband was wearing. No problem, I said. I called upstairs and made a request for the trousers of Mr. So and So. We waited and waited. Finally, I excused myself and went to see what the holdup was. It seemed that Mr. So-and-So wasn't wearing any pants anymore. All he was wearing was his underwear. "Ummm ... that's funny," I thought.

The Boss called up the old man, and within a half hour or so, he walked sheepishly in, with the pants. The family never knew.

Gory Movies

There are a lot of accidents, mutilations and all kinds of tragic deaths that the undertaker gets to see firsthand. I have seen heads blown all over the wall and only a torso lying on the floor. I got so used to seeing these things that when I'd go to the movies I was a pretty good judge of realism in the death scenes.

In the old days Hollywood did a terrible job filming death scenes. They all looked fake. I would tell my friends sitting next to me, "Now, that ain't real at all. It looks more like this." And, I would describe to them what it SHOULD look like. Hollywood must have heard me and hired an undertaker because the death scenes look a lot more realistic, some even too realistic, to me now.

Talking About Death

Why is it, when I am at a party or having a drink at a bar, or enjoying a nice dinner, the subject of conversation always turns to discussing death?

It's simple curiosity, that's why. Some people are afraid of death. And others want to know what goes on behind the big green door at the end of the hall.

Some folks are overly morbid, and want to know all the grisly details. Well, I know how to kill time, and I can gross out the best of them over a beer, meal, whatever or whenever, with stories and descriptions of how serious death really is. So I would.

If you ask a question, don't be afraid of the answer. It still happens to me.

One time at a restaurant, over beers and lunch, I was with my two cousins and we were talking about autopsies. Well, we really got into it about how the head is cut open, the brain is removed and sliced up, and how the stomach is opened and the guts are all moved about and examined.

There were two ladies sitting at the next table, and they overheard us, and they just about threw up. They asked us to change the subject, because we were ruining their lunch. We denied, because we were really into being gross. The two ladies got up and left, and they must have told the manager. Soon afterward, the manager asked us to change our topic of conversation.

One of Two

I was the only biker undertaker I knew until I started Mortuary College. Two days later I met another undertaker who rode and we rode around together. We would skip class and ride to the local bar, eat, drink and play pool. All I had for transportation for the first quarter was my Harley. Then, I bought a car.

It was wonderful to be an undertaker and biker in a college with a cosmetics program and a hair styling school. There were lots of girls.

The school covered a bit of acreage, and had a hill with a pond at the bottom. In the spring a ramp would be built and each school department would build a buggy of some kind that would be ridden down the ramp into the pond. Points were awarded for design and for going the farthest. We undertakers had a casket, attached wheels to it, and some joker rode it off the ramp. I hope they still have that party there.

My first two weeks of the first quarter in school I was doing very well. I made good grades. I hadn't yet met and been corrupted by the other bikers also going to college. After that point in time my grades dropped a bit as my time in class and studying went out with the wind through the window. Riding with the boys, playing with the girls WAS, and IS, important.

In mortuary school, each student needed to complete an 11-credit internship and work at a funeral home. Some of the boys in school hadn't even seen a dead body. Others had worked for little while in mortuaries. This internship was geared for those people.

In some states a person could not work at a funeral home without first going to mortuary school. I thought and still think that is wrong. This ain't picking up apples, honey.

If you are not given the chance to get a feel for dead bodies, how do you know you're going to like feeling dead bodies?

By first leaving everything, and moving sometimes your whole family, lock, stock and barrel to a new town so you can try your hand at mortuary school? That's right.

What happens if, after the first day, you hate it? Well, then, you have just wasted your time, the school's time, and spent a whole lot of money. There are quite a few folks out there who "tried it and thought they were going to die."

I had the opportunity to work first, and then decide.

I was the only one with around 5 years of apprenticeship already under my expanding belt. I appealed this requirement just to fill this void in my curriculum.

I had a job, it was waiting for me and I didn't feel the need to waste my time in a job that would use up my free weekends. The instructor bitched and bitched but, finally, said it was okay, as long as I filled in the 11-credit void. I signed up for an EMT-course.

Heroes

An Emergency Medical Technician. It was a great idea! I had just learned all the anatomy of a body, so it went very well. Hell, at one time I could name all the arteries and veins a drop of blood would travel through from a finger to a toe. Whoopee!

I also met a great looking girl with hair down to her butt, and she liked me.

As an Eagle Boy Scout, a person, and a biker, I have always dreaded coming up on a accident and not knowing what to do should I find someone not quite dead, and needing quick medical assistance.

So this was a great class and I enjoyed most of it. The majority of the class dealt with memorizing appropriate techniques for saving lives.

We had several classes where a student was placed in a wrecked car and we would practice having to extradite them, and put them in the ambulance. I say I enjoyed most, because, as part of the class training I had to work in an emergency room and ride around in an ambulance.

My first trip in the ambulance was the deciding point in my life.

I realized I didn't want to be an EMT.

We had received a call that a kid was choking. The address was, such and such.

I was sitting in the back of a new ambulance. A new EMT was driving and the experienced hand was in the passenger seat giving driving instructions on the best way to get to the house, without getting us or anybody else killed in traffic.

The driver was terrible. He couldn't drive a straight line if his life depended on it. We were swerving around cars, and we drove right past the street where we were to turn. We turned around and when we arrived, I was told to grab some boxes and equipment, and off we ran to the house. The old hand assessed the situation, and solved the problem in 30 seconds. I barely made the door.

A small child had swallowed a coin and was choking. The old boy just laid the small boy over his knee and slapped him on the back. Pop! Out came the quarter, and the kid was fine. We drove back to the station and waited for the phone to ring again.

I didn't like the stress of going from zero to full speed to the scene, then 30 seconds later you were trying to save a still living and flopping, in great pain, Person.

I liked it better when I was going to pick up the dead. A lot less stress. You could get lost along the way.

It isn't a matter of life and death to the dead, if you're five minutes too late.

I was in the emergency room when the ambulance brought in a woman who had crashed her car. She had a crushed hip, and some other broken bones, and was not in a happy mood. I tried to make her comfortable with some pillows. That was all I was allowed to really do. She was in pain and it pained me to see her in pain.

I decided then and there to remember the training and forget about being an EMT.

About twenty years later I was accepted and graduated with honors from a two year X-ray College.

I hadn't changed a fucking bit. I still didn't feel comfortable dealing with people in pain. I should have dropped out the first second I left the hospital on the second day.

I never worked a day as an X-ray tech; although I pay my student loan every month.

My hat goes off to ALL the people who deal with ill and dying people. It takes a lot of courage and a special personality to sit and hold a conversation with someone who is just about to die. It also takes a knack to get past the stress of a dying person right there in front of you while you do your job.

You save them. I have known many people who did this for a living. You have the gift. Thanks be to you.

Lost in Space

Many times responding to the call of the dead we would get lost going to the house. This could occur during the day, but more often in the middle of the night. There have been more than a few residents, woken up at 3 or 4AM by the knocking on their front door. They would open the door wondering what the hell is going on, and see me, all dressed up in my Sunday best...

- Um, excuse me, is this the Jones residence?"

- "Nope, they live 3 miles further up, past the creek, right at the fork, left after the bump, next to the cow field you'll see a big rock, granite I think, well, past that on the left is their house. Can't miss it. They're ma is living in the trailer now, behind the house, so she'll be in there."

They knew in an instant who we were and who we were going to get. They are neighbors ya know.

Please put you house numbers out. We can find you, unless you don't want to be found.

If that's the case then no bitching on how long it takes us to get to ya.

This has to be a real bitch for the ambulance folks too.

The family is usually waiting for us outside. Somebody has to say; "Here they come."

It's very easy to spot a black hearse slowly cruising up the street, so they walk out into the street and flag us down.

Sometimes, we can see the house we're looking for from miles away. It's easy, when it's the only house at 4AM that is lit up like a Christmas tree.

If the house has the porch light on, along with all the rest, if there are 17 cars parked haphazardly, in the driveway, the yard and on the sidewalk, you can bet money, there was something they all came to see. Now they don't want to look at it anymore and they are waiting for us, the smoother movers, to take it away.

We would quite often get some strange directions to some far away place on some distant planet.

I would get directions like this, from very excited people at 4AM. Some of them would get very upset when I would ask politely if they could repeat the directions. It didn't help matters much, that it WAS 4A.M. and I was listening still half asleep 5 minutes into their directions.

Just like the Canadian Mounties, we always brought in our man.

Because we were a busy funeral home, we would carry two cots in the back of the station wagons. In the middle 80's we switched from station wagons to Suburbans and vans. These provided a larger degree of privacy for both the dead and the living. These rigs were nondescript.

Now we could stop and have lunch or dinner or check out the new cars at car dealerships and motorcycles without anybody knowing who we were. These vehicles were also larger, and could accommodate two or three cots if needed. Many times we would need all three cots before we got back to the funeral home. Some funeral homes have vans now that have shelves in them and can carry four or more bodies at once.

We hauled 28 bodies in a van one time across the state.

Road Trips with the Dead

Often times we would find ourselves at three in the morning, 100 miles or more out and driving back to the funeral home. Some of the boys would crawl in the back, lie down and take a nap if there was an empty cot. I tried it a couple of times. If you didn't mind the fact that the person lying next to you was dead, and smelled, the cot wasn't too uncomfortable.

Ass, Grass, or Cash, Nobody Rides for Free

One time I took a friend with me to pick up a dead body, and we had to take a ferry over to an island. I had him crawl in the back, and lie on the cot. I even threw the blanket over him. So we wouldn't have to pay a passenger fare. He really didn't like it that much, and paid the fare on our return trip.

Several of my special friends, over the years, went on calls or attended funerals with me.

Hell, sometimes I would have to drive 300 miles, set up for a viewing, spend the night and the next day conduct the funeral, and then drive home. Why be alone? Two's company, three's a crowd they say. Unless the third guy is dead.

I have enjoyed the company of many ladies in hearses, Suburbans, vans, and the old traditional station wagon while on the way to or from a call, or a funeral.

And, yes, I did it in the hearse.

I had a 700 hundred mile round trip to make once to conduct a graveside service. I decided to do it all in one day, and a friend wanted to go along. She wanted to see the coast. The coast wasn't really in the direction we were heading, but it wasn't too far out of the way, so I said yes. We drove to the ocean, and parked the black hearse in a parking lot next to the beach.

I learned early on to remove the name plate from the rear windows of the hearse. That way people could not identify where the car was from. People were looking at us like we were from Mars. If you came close enough and looked inside the back of the car you could see the casket and the flowers, but only if you walked up close.

We stayed and sat on the beach and ran in the sand for about an hour. I had on a suit, so I took off my shoes and socks, and rolled up my slacks and waded into the ocean. She put on short shorts in the car, and walked out deeper and splashed me with water. My shirt and pants were soaked. I'm sure it looked pretty odd, to watch a guy in a suit and tie, with his pants rolled up, splashing around in the ocean with a little cutie. I bet some guys who were watching were envious.

We left the beach, jumped back in the hearse, and took off. I was an hour and a half late for the funeral. I blamed it on car trouble. On the long way home my girlfriend made the whole trip worthwhile.

I picked up quite a few hitchhikers while picking up the dead.

One time I was driving alone, heading for a church in a city about 300 miles away to conduct a funeral the next day. It was late morning, and I pulled off on an exit and stopped at the stop sign. I was just about to turn right and head for a store, as I was going to get a cup of coffee, when from out of nowhere a little man ran up to my Suburban, knocked on my door, and asked in an English ascent if I was heading East.

"Yes, I am" - I said.

"Would you mind giving my family a lift?"

I looked over his shoulder and there standing alongside the road was his wife holding a little baby about 5 months old and a small girl. Beside them were 4 suitcases, a baby carriage, and a walker.

"Jesus Christ! Ya sure got a load there!" I said. I explained that I had a casket in the back and I was going to a funeral.

"That's quite all right," he said, "we have seen many dead bodies."

What could I do? It was already getting hot out, and I felt it my duty to help.

"Get in." I said.

I gently placed their luggage around the casket, so as not to scratch it. There was only the front bench seat, so they all slid in next to me. First came the daughter, she was about 8, then the mother with the baby, and finally the father.

It was going to be hotter than hell that day. I had the windows up and the A/C on. It looked like they hadn't had a shower in a few days, and pretty soon I noticed a smell that was not coming from the back.

My old undertaker friend had taught me a trick about how to help get the smell out of a car, so I rolled down the back windows a bit, and turned up the air.

Soon enough we were chatting along. It seemed as these fine English folks were missionaries, and had been traveling around the world on their mission from God. They had left England two years ago, and they had worked in Saudi Arabia. He was a bus mechanic. She was an English teacher. They moved on to China, and then to Australia. They had arrived in the good old U.S. of A. down in San Francisco a few weeks ago. There, they had purchased train tickets and rode the rails to Canada to visit some of their friends. But, they were refused entry at the border, because they didn't have enough money to be allowed in. Now, they were stuck, baby carriage and all, hitchhiking across America.

What a vacation!

We got along fine until they started preaching about God and their religion. At that point, I said unless they quit preaching to me, I was going to stop, buy a six pack of beer, light up a joint and start telling dirty jokes. They did stop, and we continued on.

I had to stop three times for them to go to the bathroom. The daughter was wearing a Rolex watch. He said she had found it in a bathroom. Would I want to buy it? "Nope," I said, "I'm not into time."

I finally dropped them off at a very busy on-ramp, heading east, 5 hours later, in the middle of a hundred degree day. I wished them good luck.

I had, earlier that day, made arrangements to help my mother in the same town I was now in. She had dropped her car off for some service and was waiting for me. After dropping off "The Joad Family" I drove over, picked my mom up and told her the story. She had to see this. We drove back to the freeway on-ramp. They were long gone. It hadn't been 20 minutes since I had left them.

God, I guess, really was on their side.

I picked up a hitchhiker one very cold winter day. He jumped in but couldn't sit still. He kept looking back at the body. Finally, after about 20 minutes or so, he couldn't stand it and ask to be let out. It was about 10 degrees outside and we were miles from nowhere. Oh well.

I was coming back from a funeral in another state and I stopped at a store for a Coke once. A tall blond girl wearing a Bam-Bam dress came up to me and asked, in accent, if I was going north. "Sure," I said. "Would you mind giving me a lift?" "No problem," I answered, "Jump in." She went around back of the store and brought out a great big backpack, threw it in, and away we went.

This tall good-looking, Australian girl had been hitchhiking around the country for over three months. Her visa was expired and she still wanted to sneak into and see Canada. She was very friendly, and we drove back to the funeral home talking about Australia, and her adventures. I had never been anywhere at that time and was interested in Australia.

It was the end of the day when we got back to the office. All the boys stared at her while I finished up my work. I asked her if she wanted to freshen up a bit, at my house. She said yes, so I took her home with me.

We got home, and I introduced her to my girlfriend. It just so happened that my girlfriend and I were invited to dinner at her sister's house that night and she lived very close to the border.

The Aussie thought she could sneak in Canada in a semi-truck. I said there was a truck stop near where we were going, and I could drop her off there after dinner. She loved the idea. She showered, and in a few minutes off we went. We had a wonderful time together, and a great dinner. Afterwards I drove her to the truck stop. She was very friendly again, and said she would have liked to have slept with me and my girlfriend.

WOW! That got my juices flowing. I said I wished I had known that earlier, as I would have (after some more wine) suggested the idea to my girlfriend. But alas, it wasn't meant to be.

I wonder if she made it in and out of Canada.

My parents have a cabin on a lake. It was about 300 miles from the funeral home. Several times over the years I had to conduct funerals in towns or cemeteries near that cabin. I would usually arrive the day before the funeral in the hearse, passenger in the back. Then I would swim, ski, and party until dawn. In the morning I'd get up, shower, dress, and drive off to do the show.

I spent two months in Australia playing golf, riding motorcycles, getting pissed, drinking boxes of beer, and enjoying the lay of the ladies and the land. I checked out a couple of funeral homes and I bragged about that Aussie girl over and over while I was down under. While I was down under I was being taking care of down under, if you know what I mean.

I met a guy from England who had a car, and in 10 days we managed to make it from Perth to Melbourne. The boys in Perth gave me a good going away party and a lot of goodies for the way.

We went across to Tasmania on the Spirit of Tasmania, a big ferry, and spent 10 days in and about Hobart.

South of Hobart there is an old penal colony. It's called Port Arthur. It was a prison. If you were caught in the early 1800's stealing a pound of nails in London Town, you would very likely spend the next couple of years at Port Arthur, Tasmania. It's a historic area, and many of the buildings are still standing.

There is a plaque dedicated to 37 or so people that were recently killed there. Some guy had a gun and went on a shooting spree. This happened right before the 1984 Olympics in Atlanta, Georgia. While you're at Port Arthur, take the ferry ride around the Island of the Dead. I did. It's a small island cemetery, covered with headstones. The English were brutal in their sentencing of prisoners.

Who is Really Buried in Grant's Tomb?

When you buy your cemetery plot, make sure it hasn't been sold before. This might sound stupid, but it has happened.

Cemetery records consist of deeds and plots, and are sometimes very hard to read, let alone, understand.

First, there are the original records. They are usually handwritten and are very old.

Second, usually more than one cemetery sexton has worked at the cemetery over the years. Each, with his or her own hand writing style has also scribbled in the books, adding this, taking out that. Fifty years of that means some records are almost illegible.

Third, people have, over the years, changed their minds and have sold back to the cemetery or to someone else their original piece of Earth. Some people have made promises to include that Aunt Bee will be buried next to Uncle Sam. Some people will inform the cemetery of these changes, others won't.

And, finally, maybe one or two of the past sextons was a crook. This has happened. And a story I knew concerned a man, who sold many plots, many times. Many times it was the same plots he sold many times to many people. Then he headed off for Mexico. I think he is still there.

All this shit will leave the original cemetery records with white outs, scratch outs, and arrows pointing to this and that. It's very easy to mistake a full grave for an empty one when the records are a mess.

Fred the Cat

I had a cat, and for 17 years he had me. I brought him home in one of the saddlebags of my 69 Shovel-head Harley. He has been on several road trips to funerals with me. He was easy going, and he would go without a moment's hesitation.

One time, Fred and I had been at the lake cabin. I had a graveside service for some folks about a hundred miles away. We arrived on time, I'm looking sharp, and the graveside service went very well. They were nice folks.

That was the first time in my life when I was tipped. We aren't supposed to accept tips, I was told later, because we are funeral directors, we are not waiters.

I took the money.

After the funeral, and after everybody had left, Fred wasn't in the car. I couldn't find my damn cat.

Absentmindedly, I had left the driver's window partially down. I walked the cemetery from end to end, several times. I finally gave up, and very depressed, was driving out of town, when from out of the back, under the space where the casket rests came his faint meows. I was ecstatic! That was the last time I took the cat to a funeral.

Freeway Flowers

I had to conduct a graveside service out of state once. Suddenly, as I was cruising down the freeway in the left lane, my driver's side rear tire blew. The hearse went sliding back and forth a little, until I got it stopped along the left shoulder.

Shit!

The spare tire in the hearse was in the back, next to the casket. The casket, however, had to be almost removed to get the spare out from the back of the car. All around the casket were the funeral flowers and stands as well.

To make matters more interesting, when the tire had blown it ripped a hole in the gas tank, which was now leaking gas at a reasonable rate.

SHIT!! SHIT!

Here I was, sitting on the left shoulder of a freeway in a black hearse with a flat tire and gas pouring out and flowing down over the right two lanes. I had to move fast.

In both directions traffic was slowing down fast, to get a better look at me. I hastily removed the flowers and stands, and placed them alongside the shoulder. There were quite a few flowers.

It must have looked like I was having a graveside service, along the side of the freeway. I quickly rolled out the casket, and slid it over to the opposite side from where the spare was stored. I was in the back of the car, and was getting the spare tire out, when behind me a cop pulled up.

OH SHIT!

He walked up, looked, saw the hearse, the flowers beautifully adorning the freeway, the flower stands, the flat tire, the back door, open, with the casket sticking half way out, glistening in the sun, and then he saw the gas, which was now a small creek, heading across the two lanes and then asked me what happened. I told him.

He said if the gas reaches the other side of the freeway, he would have to close the road. I said "well, help me get this fucking tire changed." As fast as we could we changed the tire, put the blow-out in the back, threw in the flowers, and I got the hell out of there. When I left, the gas was almost to the other shoulder. I drove to the next exit, and luckily, found an auto parts store. I bought some fix leak stuff there, and I took off my shirt and tie, and crawled under the car and stuffed a bunch of this liquid metal putty in the split along the seam of the gas tank. It didn't stop the leak, but it slowed it down quite a bit.

I filled it up, and away I went. I arrived at the cemetery in time, and with the car dripping gas like an old man peeing, we had a very nice veteran's service.

Each member of the family got up to speak in front of the casket. This one guy used the casket to lean on. He leaned on it, and he pounded on it like it was a pulpit. After the service I called up the boss, told him what had happened, and I got to spend the night, while a service station replaced the gas tank. The next day I drove back, and we bought some new tires for the hearse.

Many years later I learned that if you have a gas leak, use a bar of soap and rub it into the hole. It will stop the leak.

Try it Before you Buy it

The next time you go and buy yourself a casket, ask the undertaker a few questions. See if he or she knows what the hell they are selling. Most should know the answers to all your questions. Others might not know Jack Shit about caskets.

Caskets are built from a host of materials. Most are built from different woods and metals, and plastic composites. Did you know that you could buy a casket built from fiberboard, which is a stronger type of paper? Well, yes, you can. You can now-a-days buy a casket in any shape or form you want, if you have the money and time. You can also buy a casket at some of the local big box stores.

Caskets come in two types: sealing and non-sealing. A sealing casket is supposed to be water resistant. A non-sealing casket isn't. Water is the main reason we have sealed caskets, and sealed grave liners. Water is the enemy.

So they say.

Several types of wood are skillfully used: Cherry, Mahogany, Oak, Popular, and Pine just to name a few. Wood caskets look warm, cozy and nice. Ask to lie down in one and see what you think. I have, and they are pretty damn comfortable.

You, however, will first have to buy it, before you try it.

If the dead person liked nature, a wood casket is the ticket. If he was a carpenter, what other choice is there?

The major drawback of wood caskets is once in the ground they tend to rot. Wood is wood and wood tends to rot, or disintegrate, no matter what. A wood casket placed in a non-sealing grave vault is your quickest way back to nature. Simple enough.

So don't sweat it. If you want a wood casket, but you don't want to rot too fast, all you have to do is buy a sealed casket grave liner.

We sell them! Just get out your checkbook.

Metal caskets are made from several kinds of metal: stainless steel, bronze, copper and regular, good old sheet metal. Metal caskets come in various gauges or thicknesses of metal. You can buy an 18 gauge metal casket or a 10 gauge one. A ten-gauge casket is thicker, will cost more and weigh more.

A 20 gauge metal casket is made from metal so thin, if you could rub the paint off, you might be able to read "Coca Cola" from the can it was made out of.

Most metal caskets look good. They are shiny, they are available in many different colors and in the ground they last longer.

I know where we can buy at wholesale a $105,000 (plus or minus) casket made from God knows what. It will be delivered almost anywhere in the USA in 24hrs. If you send a picture, they include a bronze bust of your dead head.

We'll let you have it for a cool $200,000. Now, that there is a casket! Want one? Give us a call. We would need to be paid in advance, please.

Don't bother calling if you want a casket that comes in colors that are pink and pleasant and glows in the dark 'cause it's iridescent. They don't make it.

Metal caskets, mid-priced and up, will have a super-duper sealing mechanism. They are called a sealing casket. You can tell one by looking for a black rubber gasket that wraps around with a few holes in it, along the edge. There is a crank that is used to securely close the top of the casket to the bottom.

This guarantees that you aren't getting out once you are in. Its sole purpose is not to allow any bad stuff, like dirt and mainly water, inside the casket. This is so you don't get wet and turn to mush. It is superfluous to buy a wood casket that has a hermetically sealed, unbreakable, impenetrable sealing mechanism, to keep out water. As I said before, water will quickly rot a wood casket. Remember, if there is water in the ground it will also get into a metal casket if there is a break in a seam somewhere.

I have lowered more than a few caskets in my time down into the grave and watched them float.

A non-sealing casket hasn't the rubber gasket, and closes without a special crank. It has a cheap clasp or a slide type of mechanism that keeps the lid from opening.

If you are superstitious, and think you might be buried alive, this is the casket for you.

Ask the undertaker what kind of material is used for the inside. There are several different types and they stitch it up in so many different ways, even I can't explain it. The linings come stitched in shrill, twill, pleated and plain. Also there is satin, lace, cloth and a paper type of lining. The linings come in several colors as well. Nice caskets also have bed springs and real mattresses that are fully adjustable insuring your stay will be very comfortable. Cheap caskets use shredded newspaper under an un-hemmed simple bolt of cloth. I've laid down in one, a little lumpy, but not bad.

Casket companies have come up with another type of casket, which might last forever, and be impervious to water: fiberglass caskets.

Fiberglass caskets, like plastic, are supposed to last forever. They are very light, very nice, but tend to look like a strange copy of a metal casket. They are very hard to find, however, in your local one- stop funeral shop. I think, maybe, the bigger casket companies were worried about fiberglass caskets taking over the market, so they might have bought up the patent and put them out of business. I haven't seen them in quite a few years. Fiberglass caskets were so light one person could easily move them. I think they had sealing and non-sealing fiberglass caskets, but I have only seen a few myself and can't remember.

Casket grave liners also come in two types: non-sealing and sealing. A non-sealing grave liner will allow granny to be baptized once and for all, whether she liked it or not. A sealed grave liner won't.

Paper caskets, um, excuse me, fiberboard and cloth-covered caskets came into existence with the increase in the demand for cremation by the casket and funeral industry as a whole. This way, old Digger O'Dell, your friendly undertaker, can still ask if you want to be laid out in a very economical casket, for all your friends to see, before being turned into smoke.

However, in most funeral homes the selection room held all the caskets and folks started buying the cloth covered paper caskets for burials too. The casket companies win, and the funeral industry wins. Your undertaker can now sell you a cheap casket for burial if you wish and for viewing someone who wants to be cremated.

Paper caskets do not seal. They absorb. They are the fastest way to go, faster than a wood box if you want to be worm food. They also leave a hell of a mess in the crematory. Paper caskets leave you having to pick out dozens of staples, snaps and crap separate from the bones, using your hands and a magnet.

You Bad Boy

I worked for an undertaker once who wasn't cremating the caskets that were to be cremated after the service was over.

I knew something was up. The day I started the job, the old undertaker was just leaving. He told me a story and warned me that the boss was crooked. This boy had quit, and I had just been hired as a replacement to manage a small branch funeral home. My boss ran the big shop in Biggs Ville.

He, when he was busted, made it on Paul Harvey, and he was front-page news for quite a while. I read about it in the morning paper.

That blew my mind!

I was working for a crook!

It seemed that he had been a bad boy for some time. It got to the cops and they set their trap.

So, I was helping him one day at the main branch, conduct a big funeral. After the funeral, I jumped into my '66 Thunderbird hot rod, and drove 120 miles to go drinking and get laid.

I didn't notice the 4 cop cars parked across the street from the funeral home. After I left, there was only the bookkeeper and the boss there. The cops drove up, made the arrest, and, in the back seat of a police car he went. He thought it was a fund raising type of joke.

Later that night when we had got back to her place the phone rang. He called.

"Could you please be here, early tomorrow morning? Something terrible has happened!"

"Sure" I said.

"God bless you" was what he said and hung up.

I knew right then that something had happened. Shit had hit the fan! The next morning, I went out, grabbed the paper and the story was on the front page.

The whole ordeal lasted about a year. He was guilty of 7 felony counts. He received a large fine, 30 days in jail, lost his license, and ruined his family's reputation in that town.

I stayed on during that year. We closed the branch firm I managed, I moved and began managing the main branch, where I assisted the families who were caught in the middle. Before this fiasco, it was an up-and-going Popsicle stand.

People continued to die, and used our funeral homes. But not very many.

It was easy money for me.

The owners changed the name of the place one day, and announced to the world that it was under new ownership. This was kind of true, as it did change ownership. It went from one family member to another.

They now wanted me to promote their, "under new ownership" funeral home to the churches in the area, and to the various fraternal and business organizations. I couldn't do that. It was a lie, and I didn't feel good about it, so I quit.

I helped build fences, lived in a tent with Fred the cat, played guitar and for a while worked as a chuck tender and powder monkey with a rock drilling and construction company before returning to the business of being the last one to let you down.

Box and Burn

The body must be cremated in a combustible container. That's a law, and a good one. A good, strong cardboard box works fine and is legal, unless you want something a little fancier.

In the old days bodies were put straight into the crematory, no cardboard box, no casket, no nothing. A body doesn't slide very well over bricks. It is much easier to have the body in a box. You don't have the arms getting tangled up with the sides of the crematory. It's the same with the legs. They will buckle up, never lay straight and hinder you pushing in the body. Believe me, it's a hell of a lot easier to slide a body into a crematory in a box.

In one funeral home I worked at we used a homemade pizza-styled slide that we placed the bodies onto to load the crematories. This was before the law. We called it Parker. It worked fairly well. It was made of wood, and had a handle. You would slide it using a roller of cardboard with the body on top and when the body was in the right place, you would quickly snap back the slide and the body would be left. The only problem was standing too close to the side of it when you were working. Because it was wood, a sliver would catch on your slacks and ruin them.

The casket companies, seeing a niche in the cremation market for cremation caskets, started building fiberboard cremation caskets. They built fiberboard caskets for earth burials as well.

They are built using some 300 staples. All are covered in a denim or cloth material. Some look pretty good. Some look like a cheap suit.

Water Sports

I had a guy give me a $50 tip one time. The second and only other time I have ever received a tip. His mother had died and he wanted to carry her out to the cot. He said that she had carried him as a child and it was the least he could do. That was okay with me. To me, it was a very kind act and I thought him a good man for it.

Well, as happens all too frequently in the funeral industry, she peed all over him. There isn't an undertaker worth his or her salt who hasn't had that happen to them.

We used to use cotton sheets to wrap the body in, and many places still do. All they did, though, was expand the area of piss and you still got wet. Nowadays, we use plastic sheets. With a plastic sheet, you can wrap up a body without physically touching it. No more hands and suits covered in shit, piss, blood and guts.

That is a beautiful thing.

I tell folks we use these noisy plastic sheets as a matter of public health.

Mine!

When you pick up a body, one guy takes the head and torso end, and the other takes the hips and legs, and you lift together, bringing the body close to your chest. Most of the time you rest the body against your chest for leverage as you move from where it was to the cot. A partner and I were doing this once, and my partner really got pissed on.

It was all over his suit jacket, shirt and tie. It made a big, wet bulls-eye on his chest. We put the body in the car and he went back in and talked to the family.

I sat in the car and laughed my ass off.

Then it happened to me. My partner laughed his ass off and I was pissed. The piss was still warm.

Where do Elephants Go to Die?

It's funny where and how people die. One of the first experiences I remember was back when I had just started working. We went to a house late one night. Out back of the house laid this old man who had taken a shotgun and blown his head off. He was lying in his back yard next to, and all over, his rose bushes.

He had planted those a long time ago, his daughter-in-law told us. We took him back to the funeral home and I started to undress him. Inside his shirt pocket was a business card. It read "Pearl's Piss Palace Nursing Home" or something like that. On the back was an appointment for him at 11 AM the next morning. Well, it looked to me, he didn't like the idea.

Watching the Living Steal from the Dead

We had a mirror placed in the corner of the hall where the main visitation room was. It was there so we could watch what people do during their visitation. Most people talk or confess, cry and laugh, and try to make themselves feel better. That is what it is all about, and that is good. A few times however, we caught people stealing rings and necklaces.

Oh yeah, that happens, and when it does, who is going to know who stole the ring? The dead won't tell, and it only takes a second to remove a necklace or ring. My co-workers and I would always watch over a visitation when the dead wore any jewelry.

If and when we noticed something unusual, like the visitor was leaning over inside the casket, it looked suspicious. You can look, you MAY touch, but you ain't stealing from us. If it looked like they were pulling off a ring or removing a pin or a necklace, we would walk in and ask if there was anything wrong. We have caught people in the act of stealing several times, and prevented it from happening. Usually the person is very embarrassed, and we ask them to leave, and they do. I have heard all kinds of stories from these people, trying to explain why they were taking the jewelry. 'It was supposed to be given to me, before she died'. Or, 'It's, mine, I just loaned it to her' they say. "Yada, Yada, Yada," I say, "Hand it back to me!" I know now what it must be like to be a traffic cop, with all the excuses I've heard.

I have never had to call the cops.

If the funeral home were to lose a ring, we could, and probably would, be sued to death. We used to talk about it and we decided, if we ever get sued, we would just hand the family the key to the place and walk out. It's much easier, and faster. Funeral homes have lost rings and other things, and when they do, it's a real bitch. Funeral homes deal with a lot of jewelry. We honestly try not to lose it.

Gold!

Lots of it.

It used to jam up the industrial meat-grinding machine we used to pulverize the bones with!   The machine made a ton of dust, but worked fine.

Every day someone had to fill up five to ten urns. This means: sweep out the retorts, take the five to ten individual pans full of dead people bones, run a magnet over them, pick out the plates, screws, bullets, and what-have-you, run them through the meat grinder, and put them into their respective urns. Then he had to label the urns, record it in a log, and place them on the shelf. The folks in some of the pans were cremated during the previous night and had cooled down.

On one of my first days, when I was on that duty, the meat grinder had bound up. That usually meant a piece of metal needed to be removed from the guts of the machine. I asked the old man watching me reassemble the machine if these pieces of metal I had found in it were gold. He threw one in the can, turned, and secretly slid the other into his vest pocket. "No" he said.

At the end of the table was a big garbage can. All the prosthetic-type of crap went into it. What else went into that can is nobody's business.

A crematory is a funny place.

Because most old crematories are lined in brick and brick uses mortar, crevices and cracks appear below where the body rests. Little pieces of little things find their way into these cracks and can stay put for a long time before being jostled loose by the broom weeks later. Read the fine print in the cremation authorization form.

One fellow swept out a small round plate of gold- and silver-colored metal. It looked like a small pile of cow shit. It was very heavy. Nobody knew it was in there. It just came out one day. Finders, keepers, but keep your mouth shut.

I heard a story about an undertaker once. He had an anniversary coming up, and he wanted to give his wife something special. He wanted to give her a new diamond ring, as a sign of his love and devotion. He bought a diamond and took it to a jeweler. He pulled out of his pocket some gold pieces and asked if these could be turned into a ring. 'Sure', said the jeweler, 'No problem. Come back in a week'. A week or so goes by, and he comes back. He gets his ring, and notices that the diamond has been changed. A smaller diamond sits in the new golden ring. He turns in the jeweler for theft, and the jeweler turns the undertaker in, for using dental gold. So there ya go.

Bad Luck

During my first month on the job, I picked up a trucker who had died. The cause of his death was listed as an accident. The state had just opened this new highway that descended at a steep angle into a city about 150 miles south of us. The old highway was a series of twists and curves that would make a snake sick. This new highway was straight with a single sweeping turn back which brought everyone into and out of the valley. Well, along comes this trucker who realizes, as he drives down the grade, that he has no brakes. No problem. This grade has a truck runaway exit. He probably is a bit worried but heads for the runaway exit. He hits the ramp, really rolling. The ramp, which is supposed to be full of thick gravel to stop trucks, isn't, and he flies off the end without slowing down a bit. It seemed the state had not used the proper type of gravel, and it had frozen. That poor trucker probably had the same thoughts of an Olympic ski jumper going through his mind.

Show Some Respect

A colleague of mine had a lady come in to claim her husband's urn. She signed for it in a register book we kept records in, and was escorted to the front door. The door was then opened for her. She walked out, down the two steps, and stopped on the sidewalk near the street. She then set the cardboard urn down on the sidewalk and kicked it into the street. When it hit the street, it broke open and the cremated remains flew all over the place. She turned to my colleague, and said, "I've wanted to kick him in the butt for 10 years," and she walked off, just like that. Cars were driving around, over and through this small pile of man, and the wind was blowing it around. My colleague, after pulling himself together got a broom and a dustpan, and quickly swept up the remains. He poured them back into the broken container and brought them back inside. He taped up the container and put it back on the shelf.

I bet they are still in storage somewhere in the funeral home. Can you believe that?

The Stairway is Job Security

It's funny to me that most of the 50 to 75 or so funeral homes that I have been into have lots of stairs. There are stairs to climb to get into the place, and stairs to get out.

There are usually stairs to negotiate getting up or down into the casket-selection room. Most of this can be explained with the age of the funeral homes. Most have been around since the town they are in was founded.

Stairs look impressive from the street, especially when they lead up to a big, clean, gothic-looking building, all white and shiny. These buildings looked so peaceful, so dignified, so somber, and so damn respectful that people just ran up those stairs, if they were lucky enough, to have their funeral there. Funeral homes have to be nice-looking.

You wouldn't take your dead mother to a crappy-looking funeral home would you?

Handicapped access became law, and a good one, in the seventies or eighties. Every new building built had to provide easy, handicapped access in, out, and all about. Funeral homes were not exempt. A perfect funeral home, I thought, would be one where you didn't have the public use stairs.

I have, with help, carried many a person in a wheelchair, up and down stairs, and into and out of funeral homes and churches. There never was a problem. We never dropped anyone or let go of the wheelchair. No one ever bounced down the stairs. You helped the elderly with stairs.

The handicap law also requires that if you remodel your funeral home you must bring it up to code by including handicap restrooms, special ramps, wide doorways, and maybe elevators. All this costs a hell of a lot of money.

I now know the reason many funeral homes have stairs: job security.

Stairs are a path to job security for funeral homes. Think about it. Who comes to pay their respects to the dead? The majority are nearly dead, that's who.

What better way is there than using the tried-and-true system called "stairs" to innocently insure yourself continued business?

Every time you help push, pull or drag all those dear old folks up the stairs into your funeral home and into your office; every time you take them up or down more stairs so they might buy more stuff. You are securing your job security.

While they are gasping and wheezing and can't focus, you sign them up and get the money. When they have finally caught their second wind, you, with all the dignity and respect a good funeral director should possess help them gently and safely down the stairs outside and, for the entire world to see, you walk them to their car. I opened their door. You are a perfect gentleman, a kind businessman, and caring undertaker. They walk away holding their chest.

If you can get them through your front door once, they'll probably be coming through your back door next.

Good service is the best policy for continued business, no doubt about it. Stairs just speed things along a little. If you don't believe it, tell me why then so many funeral homes, insurance companies and hospitals still have so many???

Some say stairs keep you young.

One time my boss yelled at me because I had a carpenter install a handrail into a brick wall, next to the concrete stairs outside. I was told that the money could have been used for other projects. Well, the stairs were slippery when they were wet, and having the handrail there made it much safer. It was a good project and a nice improvement. I told my boss he couldn't use it.

A friend of mine told me this story:

One time when he was a boy he asked his father: "Dad, why aren't you going to your best friend's funeral today?" His dad replied: "Because, he ain't coming to mine".

Men's Suits and Shoes

Once, my colleague and I walked through a department store pushing a cot. We had parked at the wrong loading dock next to the hospital, got on the wrong elevator, and got off, unbeknownst to us, on the wrong floor: Men's suits. The hospital was still 3 floors up. People waiting for the elevator were looking at us. When we walked off the elevator I thought we had screwed up. When we hit the shoe department I knew for sure that we HAD fucked up. A Hospital wouldn't have its clients coming through the men's shoe department to get to its front door. My colleague had actually shopped there and knew where another elevator was, so away we went. We got to the elevator, and laughed at what we had just done. We got our man, and went back out to the car the correct way.

Just Leave It with Me

I have had people ask me to place all kinds of unusual things in the casket with them, for them or on behalf of them. From guns to dirty magazines, from drugs to money. I have done each thing honestly and properly. I lit all the joints I could when no one was looking, to get them going before passing it over to the dead guy and sticking it in his mouth.

Hey, I was instructed by the family to do this! Someone had to get it going, didn't they? I have once taken a pull off a bottle of whisky that was going to be cremated with a friend before I flipped the switch. I don't want any bad Karma hanging over my head! You could call these on the job benefits. A Bonus, if you will. The only time I saw money left in the casket was during Asian funerals, and I wasn't going to mess with them.

There was a story about a son repaying his debt to his dad by putting a check in his dead dad's suit pocket.

It's My Funeral and I'll Play What I Want

We had a funeral for a very young man. He was about 19 or so. Before, during, and after his funeral we were asked to play his favorite music. We played a song by Elton John "Funeral for a Friend" "Stairway to Heaven" by Led Zeppelin and some other rock songs. They were loud and exactly what the family had requested. An old man in attendance stormed out of the chapel during the middle of the service. He exclaimed that he had never been to such a disrespectful funeral in his life.
I replied it wasn't his funeral.

For kicks, when a funeral was going on in our chapel, I would stand in the lobby and throw the couch pillows at my partner standing on the other side. He would in turn throw them back at me. I don't think the folks in the chapel ever caught us, but I think a minister or two saw us. We also used to mess with the reader board on the wall. It listed the names of the owners, and us undertakers. We would change our names into names like Herman Munster, Elmer Fudd, Boris Karloff or I. Emma Witch. Anything that sounded funny or morbid. Most people never noticed, but once I heard one lady ask one of my buddies if we really had a Mr. Munster working here.

OOPS!

I showed up at a funeral one time and I had placed the person in the wrong casket.

We arrived at the church an hour and half early, as usual, to set things up. The family arrived shortly thereafter, and I was quickly, made aware of the mistake. The son noticed the casket which was still in the car, and like greased lighting that Cadillac hearse and I flew back to the funeral home, sliding to stop in the garage. We quickly corrected the mistake, and arrived back at the church 10 minutes before the start of the funeral.

Everything went all right from that point on until... Wouldn't ya know it?

The cemetery had dug the grave in the wrong space, and down she went. Because the ground around a grave is almost always covered with fake grass so you don't get your feet dirty, nobody noticed the mistake. The cemetery had a tent set up too. After the graveside service everybody left and the cemetery crew filled in the grave, and at 5PM went home. The family came back later that evening, and when they saw what had happened, Oh Shit!

I guess when things go bad they go really bad. Lucky for us, the family was very understanding, or two more people, me and the cemetery man, would be looking for work. The next day they opened the right grave, corrected the mistake and we breathed a sigh of relief that that one was over.

So Sue Us

We are the only industry, I think, that can be sued for emotional and/or mental distress. A person can, and has, sued a funeral home for hearing something over the phone thousands of miles away about their dead relative that was so terrible they just couldn't live a normal life ever again. Maybe the hair wasn't combed right or there was a bloodstain on the clothes or they got put in the wrong box. It doesn't have to be much. Someone came up with the joke, if they threaten to sue, just hand them the keys to the place and walk out laughing.

The lawsuit usually involves a lot of money. In that case the dead person usually becomes their favorite relative in the world. Although they haven't seen or heard from them in 20 years, they still just loved the shit out of them and how could you tie the wrong knot on his tie? Comb his hair the wrong way or leave that stain on the shirt? How could you?

We didn't do it on purpose, that's for sure.

Now, because of what they have witnessed they can't sleep, they can't eat, and they can't think. Hell, they can't even function as a human being any more, knowing that their dear old Joe was laid out for viewing and he had on brown shoes instead of his lucky and favorite black shoes, or a blue suit, instead of black, or that his hair was combed wrong. They need lots of money from us to help return them to society, and we usually give it to them too. I can see suing funeral homes for a really big fuck up, say, losing a body or burying or cremating the wrong body.

If we screw up that bad, you should be able to get some money, and try to buy back some normality.

You wouldn't think parting the hair would be that difficult would you? Just rinse, wash, rinse, and comb. Right? Right. Now tell me sir, which side do you part your hair on? Oh yeah, you're dead. I think it's parted on this side. Oops.

I did that once and boy I felt the wrath of Khan come down on me: "How could you be so stupid, He never wore his hair that way, can't you see the natural part in his hair?" This lady went nuts. And I know Nuts.

I felt like saying to her after she had yelled at me for 10 minutes that I had asked him which way he parted his hair, but he wouldn't tell me. But I didn't. I corrected the mistake in 5 minutes.

Yes, it was my fault, but did we really, just for that, have to give the family the funeral for free?

I have tied the wrong knot in a tie on a guy before, and put the wrong dress on a lady.

Some people bring me the oldest rags you can image to dress their loved dead ones.

I kid you not. Some of these clothes are so dirty that I wouldn't use them to wash my car with.

And, of course, the dress we usually receive is a size 8. She now wears a size 10.

We have ways of making adjustments to clothes to make them fit better, but when a suit or dress arrives with a stain half the size of Texas on the front, or is 4 sizes too small, and missing half of the buttons, we're kind of screwed. All we can do is call the family, and request some different clothes. Most times that is very inconvenient for them, making a second trip back. For us it's just part of the job, because, as most people don't realize, undertakers work 24 hours a day. We will dress you in whatever we get.

Here is how it goes:

When you have had a death in your family, you need an undertaker. You usually want him to come to your house and pick up a dead body. Next, you will want to set up appointment that is most convenient to you to meet this undertaker and set up the time for the visitation, funeral, cremation or what have you. And you want it on a certain day and hour and place. "Right O", we say, and you have your funeral.

Want to Know the Rest of the Story?

Well, it has been my experience that, as death knows no time, and that there are more hours in a day from 5pm to 8am, than there are from 8am to 5pm, undertakers are usually working throughout the night as well as working all day long.

Little does this family who I am with at 2AM know or care that I haven't been home since 8AM yesterday morning. Little should they care that I have two bodies to embalm, get dressed and into their caskets, and two more to cremate. The fact that we have three funerals tomorrow doesn't come into their mind at all. It shouldn't. They want their funeral whenever and wherever, and our job is to make it happen.

It's hell on us. Most undertakers work long, uncertain hours and all have had their lives, relationships, and marriages disrupted because of it. There is a statistic that shows that many undertakers are divorced because of the business we're in.

Imagine, it's Christmas day, your wife has been working in the kitchen all day preparing a feast for you and your family; people maybe she doesn't really like but has to put up with, because of you. Two minutes after they show up, presents in hand, to eat, drink and try to be merry, the phone rings, the pager vibrates, and you have to go to work. She's left to entertain.

Well, she knew that going into the marriage. But still, she would say, "Can't they wait?"

Holidays

On Christmas day, I have gone to nursing homes, hospitals, and houses and picked up dead men, women, and children. When I have to pick up a child, man, let me tell ya, that's a tough scene. Very, very sad.

I picked one fellow out of the Christmas tree.

Sometimes getting a call is a blessing. I have used it a couple of times to get out of bad dates. I had earlier called up the answering service, when I knew I would not want to be at the place I was going to be and ask them: "Will you please call me at 7pm tonight?" "OK," they say. And when it rings, there's my excuse. "Sorry Honey can't stay here with you and your gal pals anymore. I got to go to work! Love ya. Bye." And away to my bar I would go.

Build It and They Will Use It

A man built his daughter a really nice wood casket and we had a very nice funeral. He took his idea further, and he built caskets and I bought them for many years. They were really nice, and looked swell. When he came to me with this idea, we copied the measurements from a regular casket, and he built a copy. He was able to order the same material for the lining, as well as the hinges. Because they were made local, and looked great, I talked them up. They sold like hotcakes!

I knew another guy who came to me during this same time with his homemade caskets and wanted me to sell them. I took a look and ask how much. He said a grand, and I laughed him right out of the place. His caskets looked like a cheap wooden shoebox. They were poorly made and the lining looked like it was made from an old dress. I showed him the other local casket I sold, told him the price I paid for it, which was about half of his price, and showed him the door.

Only two other times have people built a casket for their family.

Both caskets were built very well. The very first casket was made by a friend for a friend out of apple wood from the apple factory the dead fellow had worked at. It was very nice and simple with a shiny polish. A friend of a friend had purchased a nice brass plaque which had all the information nicely etched on it. It was glued to the top of the head end of the casket. Everything looked fine and the service went very nicely. If the name of the fellow had not been misspelled, the whole show would have been perfect.

The other custom casket was too wide to fit inside the grave liner. We all found this out at the cemetery, when the pallbearers placed the casket on the grave. Luckily, good spirits were all about and working through the tears and the laughter we made the necessary adjustments and properly laid this legendary man's father man to rest.

It Never Fails

It never fails when it is your weekend off. It's Friday afternoon, about 4, the boss is long gone and you are already planning to meet your friends at the bar for a drink or three and go out riding. At 4:30 the phone rings and... Poof... out the window go your weekend plans. It's another call. You take care of it, and now its 5:45PM, everything is done, your buds are waiting on you, and you're really ready to leave. The phone rings again.

"Can you help?" the boss will say "Just to meet with a family on Saturday? It will only be about three hours?"

"Okay" you say. Then Saturday afternoon the phone rings again and you end up stuck there working on your weekend off.

Here is one that is better yet. It's Friday afternoon, your weekend ON, the phone rings and rings and rings, and you spend most of the weekend, in the preparation room up to your elbows in blood and guts, needles and thread. In the old days most undertakers worked for a salary, all the night and weekend work was part of the deal.

I can't think of a better way to spend a weekend. Can you?

When you work 60 hours a week you sometimes are very sleepy. You take naps to keep going during the middle of the day or the middle of the night. Twice in 23 years, when I have been asleep I have gotten a phone call to go somewhere and pick up some dead guy. I have hung up the phone, and rolled over and gone back to sleep. Both times I have had a second phone call wondering where the hell I am.

Working is good for my drinking. It is one of the only things you can do in moderation. To count the times I have left to go: drinking, for a walk, to dinner, floating down a river, get laid, a movie, or a motorcycle ride, only to be paged that I have a call, would be impossible. Drinking in a bar is easy. For me it is a favorite, social, pastime. And it's close to work.

When I am at a bar, usually my local one, all my friends are there. They all know what I do for a living and understand when I have to suddenly leave, mid-drink, to go to work. They usually partied on, and were still there when I came back.

Sometimes a call only takes a few minutes. You get the call; you get in the car and go. If the family tells me they want this person to be cremated, that means less work for me. I drive back to the funeral home and put the body in the cooler, do some paper work and zoom back to the bar. If the family wants the body embalmed, that means more work for me. I drive back to the funeral home, embalm the body, do the paper work and then I can go back to the bar. By then, though, I'm tired, it's late, and all I want to do is to head for bed.

Necrophilia

I can't count how many times after someone hears what I do for a living, I have been asked: "Do you actually *touch* dead bodies?" Some people are so stupid I can't imagine how they got to be so old.
To the really stupid people I usually say "Oh, heavens. No! We have robots and computers that do all that stuff for us. Why! I wouldn't touch a dead body if my life depended on it!"

Some people actually believe it.

Other people have amazing stories to tell me. This is the classic story I have heard from about 20 people. It goes sort of like this;

Look, my Uncle George's friend Ted worked in a funeral home. George and me were drinking at the bar one time and in walks Ted. George buys Ted a beer and later Ted asks us if we want to see a funeral home. "You bet!" we said. So we all piled into George's pickup truck and drove up to the back door. Ted took us on a tour. I saw all the coffins in the coffin room, and the other stuff. In fact, I saw it ALL. Next, Ted took us into the embalming room where you suck out the guts. There was a dead body lying on a table. We were standing there and all of a sudden it SAT right up!" They go into more details about their tour as I sit, listen and yawn.

"Wow!" I say, "You're very lucky."

I have never seen a body move once, and I have personally handled thousands. I don't think they do move, but I don't disagree with the folks who tell me about seeing it anymore. I just nod my head, and act amazed at their good fortune.

There are amazing stories about undertakers having sex with dead bodies. I heard one during the early 1980's about a female undertaker who was caught fucking a dead guy in a hearse. Some friends made me a T-shirt 24 years ago with the words NECROCLUB on the front. On the back is a picture of a female lying on a table under a sheet. The words BE STILL MY LOVE are written over it.

I got into a fight once with the host of a party my friend invited me to. It was over how to embalm a body. He said that the blood was sucked out of the body through an artery in the foot. I tried to explain how I was taught in mortuary school, but he knew better than me. You COULD embalm the body using vessels in the foot, taking the blood out from a vein and putting in embalming fluid in an artery there, I explained, but it would be like draining the oil from a car motor through the dip stick; i.e. it would be very slow and very inadequate. Some friend of his, who had also worked in a funeral home, had told him how the embalming was done. He would not listen to my side of the story, nor to logic or reason, and he soon got pissed with my drunken arguments. My friend and I had to leave his house in a hurry, otherwise risk being beaten up. This was a bummer, as it was a great party.

How Do You Do That?

That is another question I am asked often. Embalming a body is quite a straightforward operation. All you do is replace the blood with a chemical solution that is supposed to stop or at least slow down the normal decomposition of the body. Normally an embalmer will use the Carotid artery and the Jugular vein in the neck to do the job. Using these two vessels will suffice for most fresh body embalming. Sometimes the body is not so fresh and we have to resort to pulling out arteries and veins from the arms and the legs to get the fluid into them. This takes more time, and thread, as we have to sew up all the holes.

Using the tricks of the trade poorly we can fill you up with enough embalming fluid that it will run out your mouth. This will make you as hard as a rock for a while. After the funeral, this body of yours, we bury in the ground. Once underground, your chemically-pressurized body lies there and slowly leaks into the water system, polluting the water that every single living being on this planet depends on.

And we do this by the thousands, each year.

Thereby making us, the embalmers, of great scientific importance to future generations. For, it is we, who are responsible for chemically polluting the ground water and forever changing the natural process within the world order of life and death.

The embalmer's 30 seconds of fame.

Man! That sounds important to me.

Yea right?

Yea right! It is important!

Want my advice? Don't drill a well downhill from a cemetery. At least, if you do, have it tested. In Poland and other Eastern European countries, there are many wells contaminated with Formaldehyde from old cemeteries.

Now as to the next question: Why do we embalm? Why? That's easy. Families ask us to.

I learned in Mortuary College that embalming all started back with those Egyptian Kings and Queens. The Pharaohs were embalmed.

Maybe they learned embalming from outer space, I don't know, but that is where the whole idea started. Those old boys did a good job back then. They would open up the body, remove the organs, suck out the brains through the nose, and put all the organs into clay urns. They used all kinds of herbs and spices to preserve the organs and the bodies. You can watch on television shows and see for yourself the condition of the bodies that are thousands of years old. I saw them in Egypt. Not too bad looking, for a 4,000-year-old dead guy. They did a very good job, and did it without embalming machines, a custom-tilting table, or a specially-ventilated room. I bet they didn't even use gloves. I toured the Valley of the Kings in Luxor Egypt, and saw clay urns, and other interesting things.

Embalming was, however, forgotten for the most part, until the end of the Civil War.

It was then that this guy who had been studying dead bodies figured that if he could exchange the blood inside the body for some preservatives, the dead body would not go rotten so fast. Maybe, by doing this, it would give dear old Confederate mom and/or a Yankee dad some time so they could come and see their son, the dead solider.

It worked. And it started a small ball rolling in the change of the disposal of the dead.

Up until that point when you were dead, you were dead. Your family, if you were lucky, laid you out for the townsfolk to see, and then they buried you. The best undertakers (which were as rare as hen's teeth at that time) could do for you was put you on ice, which wasn't very handy at the time, and hope someone would come and claim you. The rest of the time, undertakes were dentists, carpenters, and blacksmiths.

"Yup, that's him. Yes sir. That's old Tom, all right! He smells a little worse than usual. Why is his tongue sticking so far out of his mouth?"

There was a period of time when you could buy a casket with a glass window in it. Whether it was for looking in or out, I can't say.

If you weren't sure that you were really dead, when everyone around you thought you were dead, you could be buried in a casket with a string attached to your finger. That string led up to a bell attached to your headstone. I can hear the boy saying... "Pa! If ya wake up, just ring that bell Pa! We'll fetch some shovels, and come dig ya out, quick like!!"

The funeral industry changed after the Civil War, and America was on its way to becoming more industrialized, centralized, and civilized. Undertakers started by providing the dead with respectable, dignified and expensive funerals.

After the Second World War there were a lot of veterans who came home with vast experiences in blood and guts. Most of these men went into the service as young kids, and when they came out, many hadn't any real useful skills or education with which to support a family. Many of those men went to mortuary schools and became undertakers. The funeral business boomed as did the rest of America after the war, and many of them became very successful.

Most of the boys I knew from those days are now gone. They were fun to work with. They taught me more than I leaned from mortuary school.

I wonder if they were embalmed, knowing what they know?

The mortuary schools at that time were as serious as a nun in a church. Their way was the only way. If you couldn't cut the mustard or the body, out you went. There are many schools that survive to this day that were started sometime after the war. Most schools put out good students over the years, and in the middle 1980's a mortuary school put me out on the streets.

Dying to Get In

When you attend mortuary school you learn, among other things I have already talked about, how to embalm a body. Or, at least you get to try and learn how to embalm. The school I went to didn't have a lot of people dying to get in and be embalmed by some uneducated school kids. We got our bodies the old fashioned way. We dug them up from the cemetery! Just kidding. We barely made the required limit of embalming bodies.

Where do the schools get these bodies?

Most of the schools used to get the bums and the homeless wanderers that died without any family. Nor did these people have any funds for a funeral home to profit from. So, after finding this out, local funeral homes would deliver to the school Mr. John Doe, and we would cut, slice, dice and embalm, trying to create a masterpiece of pure embalming form and function, from stinky old dead people. It was a win-win situation; the funeral home was happy, they didn't have to spend any more time or money on this fellow, and we were overjoyed with the pleasure of having such a wonderful experience.

This system worked fine for many years. The old boys would tell me stories of having to embalm hands and feet that would be found here and there. There are always a lot of people without family or funds who die, and someone needs to take care of them. You can't leave them lying around in the streets. Embalming schools are like medical schools, with respect that you can't learn to take care of bodies without working on bodies.

I worked for a funeral home that had a contract to bring the dead people to a medical school. We had to follow strict guidelines the school set up for us. No fatsos. No cancer.

It is a great idea to donate your body for medical science, just don't eat that third donut. Some people try to donate their body to get out of the expense at the funeral home. Not a bad idea, but be prepared to be turned down anyway. You are not the first one with that idea, if you catch my drift. We brought in so many bodies and saw the most unimaginable things being done to these bodies that one might not want to consider being a body donor after all.

One old undertaker once told me something a long time ago, "Never worry about the dead ones," he said, "Worry about the live ones" That made good sense to me. Now, however, things are different.

One of my instructors told me that a living, breathing, human body has millions of bacteria floating around in it. When it is dead, that number multiplies itself by 10 and 10 and 10, as the time goes by.

This means that a dead body is now more dangerous than a live one. Add to this all the new super, drug-resistant diseases we have now that just keep on living even after you're dead, diseases that we didn't have 20 years ago. Let me tell ya, I don't go picking my nose anymore after just picking up a dead guy. I pull off my gloves first.

It has come to the point that, by law, we undertakers are required to treat every single body as if it was as contagious as Typhoid Mary. We are supposed to wear special clothing every time we touch a body. We even are supposed to wash our hands as often as a doctor does.

Some guys are allergic to soap, so we have some special soap. Some guys are allergic to the latex in the gloves, so we have special gloves for them. The zoot suits we are supposed to wear are the same surgical suits the doctors and nurses wear when they operate. In a sense, we are also operating. We have to wear the booties over our shoes, the masks, goggles, pants, shirts, head coverings, and gloves. One thing they do is keep the blood and guts off your tie and white shirt. That's a bonus right there. The suits are required for a reason: mainly, our health, and that's good.

The suits, however, are hot, uncomfortable, sweaty and hard to rip off in the few seconds' time you get after the front door rings and before the husband of the dead lady on the table walks into your preparation room.

Many times I have been dressed up in this monkey suit, only to have to rip myself out of it to answer the door. You can't, for God's sake, run out and greet the visitor in this outfit. If you did, you might give them a heart attack. So, you rip off the suit, and walk out. If you're not fast enough getting out of that space suit and greeting the person, that person might start to wander around and greet you.

Having the family walk in and find you in the preparation room with your arms in the belly of their loved one is NOT cool. I have come close to being caught many times, but not quite. I usually met them about halfway down the hall. I'm usually covered with sweat, because I sweat like a pig when I am dressed up in the suit, and for having just changed back into my clothes in 30 seconds.
I'm kind of hot blooded. I sweat a lot. I can think about work and start sweating.

I must run at a little higher temperature than most folks. My boss once said so. Many times I'd be alone, working fast and furious, but calm and cool, sewing up somebody's head and right in the middle of the job, with one hand holding the hair out of the way and a needle with suture attached, in the other hand, and, God Damn it, the phone would ring or the doorbell would ring and somebody would show up. Then I'd start sweating, like some overworked horse.

If anything is going to go wrong it usually goes wrong for me in the preparation room. I admit I'm not the best embalmer in the world. I don't like to embalm. And I believe that in most cases it is not really necessary. However, the dead, if they have been dead a while, look better embalmed. So I do the job.

For me, shit will hit the fan when I'm alone. It's usually busier than the blue light special at Kmart. The phones won't quit ringing, the doorbell keeps dinging, and everything is going off at the same time. Right in the middle, there I am: shooting the juice into some dead guy, a needle stuck in his neck, a clamp here, another one there. A guy's got to be careful doing this. But, then the phone rings; information about the pallbearers for the service on Thursday; then it's the door; more flowers being delivered. It's damn hard to keep everything straight.

Let's see here... Mrs. Smith still needs to have her nails and hair done, she needs to be dressed, casketed and cosmitized. Mr. Jones needs to be embalmed, aspirated, and dressed. I need to sweep out the crematory, load Mr. Peabody in, because the family wants his ashes tomorrow. I've got to move Mrs. Cotton with the flowers from the viewing room into the chapel for her service tomorrow. Also I have a body to pick up at the hospital, two death certificates to type, and four obituaries to write and fax to the paper. I also have to change the spelling of the cousin in one obit, add the names of the pallbearers to another, plus, print up three funeral folders, and remember to find the title to that one song the Jones family wanted, how the hell did that song go..."On a hill far away..."?

An undertaker learns to put things into perspective and in some haphazard order. I manage to bring in the newly dead, get the old dead embalmed and sewn back together, and washed, and dressed and put out for show. Plus, I take care of all the paperwork.

I have had over the years some major fuck-ups, but, I fixed them all. Sometimes I needed help.
You want to know one good thing about embalming a dead person? They don't mind, when you fuck them up. And after you fix them up they don't squeal on you.

I was embalming a lady once, and the phone rang. I answered it, leaving the embalming machine pumping with the juice going into her head. Some lady wanted information about something or other. When I hung up the phone and went back to my embalming, her neck had swelled up so big she looked like she had a goiter. She could have married the Michelin Tire Man. If you don't know what a goiter is, imagine having a grapefruit stuck in your neck.

Fuck! Fuck! Fuck!

And… wouldn't' ya know it… right fucking then the boss walks in. He goes through the roof! I was shaking. I had screwed up, bad. We took a large wet towel and wrapped it tightly around her neck. The pressure from the towel eliminated the swelling overnight. The next day she looked fine. The family never knew, and thought she looked great.

We have all kinds of ways to make the dead look alive when, by all reason, they really should look dead.

Eyelashes

While I was in Moscow, Russia, I went to see their old comrade Lenin.

He is laid out in his own mausoleum. The building, which sits on one side of Red Square, looked to me like it could survive a nuclear blast. There wasn't much of a crowd that day to see him. And he only accepts visitors a few times a week. I had to wait in a short line next to one of several entrances of Red Square to get in. The Center of the Square was roped off so you could only walk around the perimeter, not like I had done the day before. To see Vladimir Lenin was free but no cameras were allowed. This really bummed out the Japanese who were also waiting in line. When it was my turn, I walked along the side of Red Square, and into his tomb, down several flights of stairs and around a few corners and into a room where he was laid out.

There were guards everywhere, all of them carrying AK47 Russian Kalashnikov machine guns. In every corner, there stood a guard. I figured they must be there in case someone decided to pick up comrade Lenin and take him home.

No, more likely they were they to keep people from destroying him, for all the evil deeds he did.

But, anyway, here I was and there was he.

I entered the room from the right side. The first thing I noticed is that he was laid out like a Pheasant under glass, in a glass sarcophagus. It was lit up like a shrine, and it was about 4 or 5 feet from a raised platform you had to walk around. You walked up some steps, down his right side, around by his feet and then walk out past his left side and down some steps and out you go.

Well, up the steps I go, and I took one look at him and noticed right off that his right eye was all fucked up. Call it, if you will, a professional habit, but Jesus! All his eyelashes on his right eye were stuck together and the makeup around that eye was smeared. Having an eye for details, I caught that right off. If Mr. Lenin had died and come to my funeral home, I would have never let him out the door with an eye looking like that. I stood and looked at his eye for a little while, and then started to walk around him.

He was lying on his back with a blanket pulled up to his nipples with just his right hand sticking out. He had on a suit and tie, and as such, looked real good except for the eye, for being dead some 80 years or so.

I walked around his feet and looked up at him and noticed, quite amazed, that the fingertips of his right hand were left blue. Where the fuck is the make up??? As I laughed at that, inattentive of my current surroundings, I felt the great presence of an AK 47 and his friend at my side. Next thing I knew, I had an arm on my shoulder from a guard who looked as serious as Lenin looked dead. This nice man escorted me to the exit immediately. I went along without even putting up a fight.

I was told they have seven or so embalmers keeping the comrade sweet and clean in his glass house just so all the tourists with morbid curiosities can come and see him. And, what a sight to see! He's been dead longer than most men have been alive!

I, I think, in my perfectly normal drunken haze, would have made his eye look better and covered up the blue on his fingertips. That's what we have makeup for. Gee whiz! Now I know why they don't allow cameras.

Very few Russians visit there. When I was there the only other visitors were European and Japanese tourists, who, like I, had brought cameras so that they could have their picture taken beside the great dead man and were depressed that cameras were not allowed.

By the way, if you want to see comrade Lenin you better hurry. I have heard that they are planning to bury the old boy in St. Petersburg, next to his family.

I bought a Kalashnikov machine gun in nice wood box while I was in Moscow. It is made of glass and holds an ever-evaporating amount of fine vodka.

I saw the old dead leader Mao, of China, while I was in Beijing. One time was enough. The Chinese keep you on your guard. You get a quick look from about 50 yards out, as you walk in a line along with hundreds through his building.

When I was in St. Petersburg I also checked out the Kunstkamera museum. There, I looked at all kinds of deformed babies. I was interested in seeing this stuff until I saw I wasn't interested in seeing this stuff. It wasn't very pleasant. Let me tell you. There were two-headed babies, Siamese twins still attached to each other, babies with arms coming out of their stomachs, and other terrible stuff. All these babies were stuffed into big jars. It was odd, but in the 1700's it was the fashion.

If you were into science, fashion, and medicine, and could afford it, you had to have one of these little items in your living room. Maybe you had it in the dining room, on the mantle above the fireplace or placed on a French table in the Parlor. If you were anybody important, you had one. Then, when you held your big dinner parties, and everybody who was anybody was there, you could pick it up, discuss its facts and features and act very important. Some people used to have mummies from Egypt laying about in their living rooms as well. It was a sign of sophistication, a short-lived, morbid sophistication.

A doctor from Holland way back in the early 1700's had been collecting these oddities. He gathered quite a collection. Along comes Peter the Great on one of his European journeys and buys them all, for some amazing amount of rubles. In the name of medicine, he brings them back for his people to wonder and gaze at.

I wondered what for, myself.

The museum was packed. It had exhibits on Native American Indians and peoples from around the world. Its displays and exhibits are world famous, and including the baby collection, it was a very interesting place to spend some time.

I could write a book about the Hermitage Museum, but somebody else probably has. That place is worth a visit.

St. Petersburg is a beautiful city. A museum in, and of, itself. The palaces, museums and churches there are un-fucking believable.

Watch Out

In the Eighties we were hit with the AIDS virus. It hit the world of the dead just as hard as it hit the world of the living.

I remember going to one of the first seminars given to the medical and undertaking professions. After the disease was explained, and the serious consequences disclosed, it was time for questions and answers. The only question that came from the undertaker section was: "How long is the virus alive in a dead host?" At that time they didn't have the answer. That shocked the hell out of us. What did that mean?

Would we now be picking up dead bodies with live AIDS? Yup. Would we be embalming AIDS bodies? Yup. This was a big issue for us in the 80's. Back then it was mostly confined as a gay man's disease, and we weren't gay. We were and still are afraid of catching AIDS from a dead body.

Worse yet, the cause of death was now also a matter of personal privacy rights, so initially undertakers were not made aware of the disease when we picked one up. That pissed us off as well. Some funeral homes in the beginning would not embalm AIDS bodies. After a few more years of study and research along came the zoot suits. I have mentioned we are required to wear them now. To the best of my memory AIDS can last 48 hours in a dead host.

Talk about a hot body!

I used to be able to tell, in those early years, just from the voice in a phone call if we were going to be going to an AIDS house. The call usually came from a male, a partner of the deceased. And no, they were not related, but they lived together in the same house. The voice was polite and soft. Most times when we got to the house, I was right.

Back then AIDS was just as scary as it is now for us, and for the nurse who pricks herself with a needle. When that happens, a thousand thoughts of life and death rush through your head. All the preventions and precautions in the world don't mean a damn thing, after you've pricked your finger with a needle working on a stranger. Does he or doesn't he have something contagious? Now have I got it?

And where do you put the blame when you prick yourself? I blame myself for it. I have cut myself embalming a body more than once and I have wondered if I have just given myself the cursed cut.

I have been tested for AIDS, T.B., and all the other bad shit that will kill the average undertaker several times, and have been lucky so far. Knock on wood.

You don't hear of a mechanic getting AIDS from cutting his finger while working on a car, do you? When a mechanic cuts his finger he usually hits the car and swears. When I cut my finger I swear and then take a hit from a joint.

Times have changed and due to better medicine and better precautions we don't hear about very many cases of nurses, doctors or other medical professionals as well as us, undertakers, getting infected from AIDS. That's good news.

The bad news is that there are many more diseases out there, lurking, in the dark, waiting to get us.

Everybody has to die. Some people don't die soon enough.

Sometimes, the bad ones live, and the good ones die early.

Why is that?

Does anybody really know what the answer is? Does anybody really care?

More Bad Luck

We picked up a lady one time that had the misfortune of being in the wrong place at the wrong time. This happens to a lot of people every day. In her case, a spare tire had bounced out of a truck going in the opposite direction, the tire had crossed lanes and had come bouncing and flying along at about 50 mph right through the windshield of her car. She had Goodyear printed all over her face.

Why did she have to die? She was a pillar in her church and an upstanding member of the community. She was heading to church when this happened. Why couldn't it have been someone else?

In my opinion, when your number's up, it's up. Now, granted, you can always increase your odds by stepping in front of a train or jumping from a plane without a parachute. Well, I have heard stories about men in the service who have survived a fall like that, but really for the most part, if you try to trump life and do something super stupid, you are on the highway to Hell.

Usually death catches most of us off guard which is fine by me.

Can you imagine living your life with a colored stone stuck to your palm that, when it glowed you knew you were about to die? Yeah sure, you say, you saw the movie, too.

Head in the Middle of the Road

Do you know that a head weighs around 20 pounds or so? I do.

I found this out when I went to pick up a biker who had gone a bit too fast on his Harley Davidson Electra Glide, the police in hot pursuit. He was doing pretty well, and he had gone quite a few miles down the freeway at break-neck speeds. But either he must not have known, or had other things on his mind or just forgot that an Electra Glide is not the best handling bike is the world. Especially, not at high speeds, swerving through and around heavy traffic, with the police hot on your tail. This is funny, as the police for many years used Electra Glides as highway patrol vehicles. Well, he pulled off onto an off-ramp way too fast, crashed, and partially flew through the guardrail. I say partially, because only his head made it. The bike and his torso were lying on the road, but the helmet was far away, the police said. His head was in it.

This is really heavy stuff, I thought.

Did you know that there are some 20 bones in the head? I had to know them all in school but have forgotten most of the names by now. The frontal bone is connected to the temporal bones the temporal bones are connected to the occipital bone. That's the way I remembered them. The mandible bone, now that's a bone you can sink your lower teeth into. Everyone has a bat bone.

Talking about the bones in your head isn't something that you bring up in conversations with chicks you are trying to get into your bed. I usually wait until after.

Girls

Some girls won't have anything to do with someone who touches dead bodies. I have had several girls shiver and freeze up when they find out what I do. It's like they refuse to identify the living from the dead. I'm alive, I would say. I even tell them that I wash my hands religiously; once a week.

On the other hand, well, some girls like guys like me. Maybe it's the expensive suits I wear or the way I swear or the classic old cars and motorcycles I own or the nice house I call home. Some girls, however, are fascinated by death. I call it morbid curiosity. Get a few drinks into them; tell them a few stories, and BAM! They want a tour of the funeral home.

I would use that as the final touch. The funeral home tour, if you will, to win them over. I would show them the chapel and the caskets. Maybe let them lie down in one, and I would show them the room where we did the embalming. I'd show them the crematory and tell them some, just some, of the tricks of the trade.

If the girls were by then, really good and hot, I would let them peek at a real, live, dead body.

After a tour by me a few would be sick to their stomachs. Most, however, would be as horny as if they just got a new lease on life, and I held the pen and paper.

Boy, those were the days my friend, those were the days.

I got old, but I never slowed down.

Where There's Smoke, There's Fire

I tried to smoke cigarettes once.

Almost everybody in the funeral home where I worked smoked cigarettes. It was I guess the cool thing to do. So I bought a pack of Marlboro lights and started puffing.

One time, as my cousin and I were driving to the funeral of our great uncle, I flicked a cigarette butt out of the driver's window because smoking it was making me sick. We were drinking and driving our way east. The next day at the funeral, my cousin and his mother showed me a hole that my cigarette had burned in his sleeve of his sports jacket. That God Damn cigarette had flown back in the car and had landed on the back seat, where his jacket, in a garment bag was laying. It burned a hole the size of a quarter! I can't believe we didn't notice the smell of burning plastic and wool…. Well, yes I can. It must have been masked over, by better-smelling smells.

Another time, I was riding back from a funeral in the hearse. I was smoking a Marlboro Light. My partner was smoking a Camel straight.

"Here" he said, "smoke a man cigarette."

"Okay," I said.

I threw my little kid cigarette out the window and lit up one of those short, no-filter kinds that he handed me. This was the brand of cigarette that all the famous dead cowboys smoked.

In no time at all I was as dizzy and woozy as Lucy Ricardo. Five seconds after that I felt a burning sensation, and looked down to see the ash which had fallen off my cigarette had burned right through my new silk tie, my nice white shirt, and was now burning a hole through my tee shirt into me. I gave up smoking cigarettes after that. Smoking marijuana, for me, tasted better and was the better choice.

I about killed my boss once. He was another smoker who went with me down some steep narrow stairs into the basement of an old house to bring out big old dead Joe. This fellow also smoked the smokes all the dead cowboys smoked. Well, we heaved and hoed this big fellow up those stairs, down the hall up onto a cot and left. I drove. He was sweating bad, and about coughed up a lung. He had a little blood coming out his mouth. He said he was fine. After a ways, he lit up.

Don't know how it happened but 10 years went by fast. I got a little fatter, and girlfriends tended to stay around longer than a few months. I was making more money, having more fun, and I had more bills to pay. Life was, for me, still very, very good.

I was able to graduate college with my second degree, from a prestigious school for the rich and famous. After 10 years, I paid off all my student loans, and had for a while a letter thanking me, and a check from the student loan association for over-paying my last student loan payment by 17 dollars. I did that on purpose and I never cashed their check.

And a Very Good Friend Indeed

I have so many friends in so many of the important professions of the world. I couldn't be luckier. When I needed them they were, and are still, there for me, and when they needed me I was there for them.

I have taken good care of many friends who have died over the years. I miss them all and stand by the fact that I did everything I was supposed to do by them. Whatever that meant doing, I did it. Some friends died by way of being just too damn ornery to live. Accidents, suicides, having too much fun, overdoses, old age, young age, a bee sting, motorcycle and car accidents, and diseases, have all claimed the lives of others. Everybody has friends who die. It's the same the world over and it's always a bummer.

For me, however, it was different. I was the undertaker who took care of things when my friends died. How many of you can say you sewed the head of your friend back together?

I was a white-collared professional, a suit and tie type, who also rode Harleys and, with my friends, lived and breathed to party. All my friends are mechanics, carpenters, plumbers, electricians, body shop repairmen, brick masons and the all-important bike mechanics. These are the blue-collared professionals who, in everyday real life really make the world go around. When your toilet is overflowing, you are in deep shit. Who do ya call?

Who misses a lawyer?

Any time I needed help with something, all I had to do is go to my second home, the bar, and look up a friend who knew more about what I needed done than I. That was easy, as I profess not to know much about fixing anything that isn't already dead.

Most folks in the suit and tie profession live in an entirely different world than I do. They drink, I hope, the same, and, God, I hope they enjoy life the same, but they probably don't know when the plumber's birthday is, the same plumber who would come to your house and replace your leaking toilet for a beer and a joint. Or the body shop expert who would, for free, repaint your saddlebag lids only because you were too stupid to put them on the motorcycle right in the first place, so they fell off, slid down the freeway, and got ruined.

The carpet guy, the landscaper, the appliance and the furnace guy, the carpenter, the electrician; all these guys are very important. Most white-collared professionals don't associate with these blue-collared people. These are the people I feel comfortable with.

I have all kinds of friends in all types of high and low places.

I have the pleasure, however, of having a few friends in high places. You know, doctors, lawyers, professors and professional folks. They get high and they get low and nasty just like the rest of us. We might not always see life the same way; we just might see it from a different point of view. They don't see it the same way as me.

I look forward to a drink. Many of them look for a drink to look forward.

I have friends in low places too. If low places means life in a bar scene; i.e. the fun zone. Well, you can usually find me in the bars, strip joints, motorcycle shops and swap meets. I live there and the people there are my friends.

Hell, I'm going to be the last one to let you down.

You can bet your life on that.

The Constant Party

Undertaking has turned me into a sort of chameleon. I don't take a side in many issues today. Nor do I enjoy a good debate. I prefer to listen in and zone out. If you want to believe that the Republican Party is better than the Democratic party, or that the Yankees will win the series over the Red Sox due to this or that player; whatever you believe, that's okay with me.

I gave up a long time ago belonging to a particular political party. The advice came many years ago, from a fellow I was sharing a joint with out in my car one day during a break between classes. He said something about the constant party being the best place to be. I agreed then, and still do. Work hard and play hard. So what the fuck, in my own mind I joined the constant party. I don't think I'm the only member. I wrote a song about the constant party.

So, if you think your dad was a no good piece of shit and you want me to dispose of his dead ass as quickly and as cheaply as possible, that is okay with me.

If your mother, however, was to you, the Virgin Mary, and you demand she receives the best money can buy, that is just fine. Just bring plenty.

My feelings were refined through the many people, places and things that have influenced my life.

First, being an undertaker. That job hammers in the nails about the simplicities of life and death. Second, the ministers to which I have listened to over the years preach about religion and dying. Their religion, they say, is the only religion, and is the best religion to die with. All other religions, they claim, won't give you a big stone mansion in the sky. Therefore, ours is good, theirs is bad they claim. I hate that shit. Whether you are religious or not you are still going to die.

Third, I blame it on the countries I have been to. Countries where life meant and still means very little, so the ruling parties killed innocent people by millions.

Finally, I blame it on my own lifestyle and the things I have done to myself. All the chances taken, like when I drive fast. It's a wonder I'm still alive.

In my mind everybody is going to die. So why not let them believe what they want to believe? They will anyway. Debating is not the job of this undertaker. Oh no, it's not my job to change people's minds. It's my job to bury the minds with the people. While the good folks of this world are alive, let them believe and fight for what they believe. When they die, let them come to me. Then, if I want, I CAN change his or her mind. If there happens to be one lying around.

Instead of a heated debate yelling over bullshit, I prefer discussing, and listening, and talking and working things out. I usually try like hell in the first place not to push the buttons of people that will bring out a debate.

It kinds of makes sense to me that I am a Libra.

Another Old Man

I worked with this old man for many years. He was into embalming. Sometimes he would embalm the penis of the dead guy until it stood up, real proud. I stood and watched.

A Little Religion Can Kill Ya

Religion. Now there's a subject any good undertaker can preach about.

Everybody is entitled to his or her religion. That is their God-given right, guaranteed by the Constitution of these here United States. I'm all for it. I can take most of the religion you may want to throw at your funeral, but leave out the Hell-bent-for-fury, if you please, preachers. They're holier-than-thou when they're preaching along during the funeral. What I'm talking about is the preaching before, and after, the funeral.

I have heard so much bullshit from preachers over saving souls, repenting your sins, and making sure you are giving the church its stipend each week, I could, after a few minutes of listening, (in my own mind) pick out the real honest minister from the placebo. Many of these preachers I met didn't know the dead person from Adam, and didn't care a damn about anything he or she did! The only thing they cared about was the check they received for their services. Now listen up.

Often undertakers get families who don't know any ministers, and therefore want us to find someone to officiate at the funeral. Maybe they are not religious, or they are new to the town, but nevertheless, mom is dead and they need some preaching done.

I heard this story from an undertaker: One time, a girl died and didn't have a family preacher. A friend of the extended family, like a friend of a cousin, said that he had a really good preacher for the service. The family, not knowing anyone else, agreed. The funeral chapel was full of bikers, and the usual bar crowd, as this was the dead girl's lifestyle. Well, the preacher came in, all fire and brimstone, took one look at this heathen crowd which had packed the place, and decided he needed to do some soul-saving. He went on and on about the evils of drinking, sex, drugs, rock and roll, prostitution, evolution, revolution, and a lot of other bullshit: the results of which will lead you straight to hell. He went on until a big biker stood up and said, "Preacher, are you going to try to save us or just condemn us all straight to hell?" And with that he walked out. So did the family and everybody else. The preacher was left alone at his pulpit to contemplate his navel. They loaded her up in the hearse and roared off to the cemetery, where the big biker talked about the girl's life. That was a good service.

A good service doesn't have to have 45 minutes of religion injected into the souls of the non-religious, still living, crowd and the dearly departed. I have stood and worked many great funerals where not a word was spoken about soul saving, clean living, or pure thinking.

I dealt with a priest once who really took the cake. It still makes me mad.

This came about because my boss had made a pre-arrangement for an imminent death with a family. He had written the priest's name down on the arrangement sheet along with the dead guy's name. That was the entire pre-arrangement. Well, the family was in from out of town and wanted a Catholic service.

The death came on a Friday afternoon, and the family wanted the service the next day.

A wham-bam, thank you ma'am, kind of thing.

They were going to transport their son in his casket themselves, many hundreds of miles back home, and have another funeral and then bury him there. So I call up this priest, ahead of making arrangements with the family, and explain the situation. "Could you help the family?" I asked. This went over like a fart in church.

He didn't recognize the family name, of course. And, he was heading for the lake Saturday. And this was really going to be a big bother for him. To preach at a funeral of someone "Who had never even darkened my door", he said, seemed to him to be ludicrous. After some more complaining, the last thing he said over the phone was that he would do the service, and that there had better be a damn good stipend in it for him. I said I would ask the family.

A stipend is money we give to the preacher for their time and service, and we include it on the bill. That's all fine and good enough. Business as usual. We do that for soloists and organists and piano players too. Some couldn't play well or sing well, but what the hell, they still got paid.

Well, later that day, I met the family and we went over the details. There were about 6 of them, I remember. I came to the part and explained the need for an honorarium for the priest.

"Yes," they agreed, "that would be nice. Would you give the priest seventy-five dollars from us?"

"Yes certainly". I said.

I knew it wouldn't be enough.

We had the funeral and everything went just like clockwork. Five people showed up. The family was happy and the priest did a good job. I had placed his check, sealed in an envelope, on the pulpit along with a list of songs I was going to play for the service. I knew that he wouldn't be able to open the envelope until after the service.

Well, not two minutes after he said Amen and the family had left the chapel for the reception room, he opened the envelope; he walked out of the chapel, stormed down the hall into the office and down my throat.

"Why! This is bullshit!" he said. "I'm not giving up my weekend for this measly amount!" I remember him saying.

He piercingly chewed my butt about wasting his time, ruining his weekend and all this shit! He went on and on and on. I finally interrupted him by saying that I think the family can hear him. That didn't matter. For seventy-five lousy bucks I had ruined his weekend. Well, he left, and I helped the family load their son into the back of a pickup truck and then, they left. That podgy padre however, had left me in a foul mood.

At least, thank God, the family didn't hear him. But guess what? It gets better.

Not long after everybody left, I was in the middle of making another funeral arrangement with a different family and the phone rang. It was the Priest! He was now well into his cups, I think, and he immediately, through slurred words, let me have it. He let go with all the bitching he could conjure up about me ruining his weekend for seventy-five dollars. He yelled at me so loud, over the phone, that I couldn't keep it close to my ear. My new family and I sat and listened to him loudly complain. Finally, I interrupted him and I said I was with a family and they can and have heard every word he had said. After that, he hung up. But before he did, he said, he was going to talk to my boss, as sure as hell.

I told the family sitting in front of me that it was a priest on the phone who was just a little upset about his stipend. The family was shocked this was a priest swearing and yelling as he was.

That next day, I bitched to my boss about his rudeness to families, to me, and the money issue.

This didn't do any good. I actually think he gave the priest a little more money. After all, you wouldn't want a priest bad-mouthing your funeral home to his congregation, would you? It's not good for business.

One time I picked up a priest who had drank too much wine in his new hot tub. The wine bottle was empty and he was floating face down, as red as a lobster. That was good for business.

A priest, in my humble and not-too-religious opinion, should accept the stipend he receives for conducting a funeral service, any amount. After all, I don't think the money entirely belongs to him in the first place. Isn't it supposed to go to the church? Isn't one of the priest's jobs to bless the dead, give them their last rights and conduct funerals? For *free*, if necessary? I don't know for sure, but I think so. From that day on I never addressed that asshole as Father So and So. I just used his name.

I have, on the other hand, seen and heard some great preaching done over the years. Really good services that almost made me tear up. No joke. Some preachers of God are blessed with a gift of talk that can honestly help other people when they really need it. Others do it to make a living. I pray the hope and good in all of us doesn't get buried over with all the things from Pandora's Box.

You can have almost anything you want said and done at your funeral. If you got the money, honey, I got the time. Just call me.

I have had bagpipes and harps played, and children sing at funerals. For money, I can arrange to have doves released, on cue, to fly high into the soft blue sky. Ah Man, It's Beautiful! It will make you cry. I have released hundreds of balloons, some with written notes of hope and love inside. So, where do all these balloons go? I know. They land downwind somewhere. Some are then eaten by animals, killing a few. The rest become trash.

At a few funerals of friends and strangers I had Harleys started up and roaring for fallen brothers and sisters. I have had a bike or two in the chapel, too.

Cat Fight

I met with a family many years ago to make arrangements for their mother. Across the desk from me, from left to right, sat the eldest daughter, her husband, then the youngest daughter and her husband.

"Simple cremation, no services," they said. "Fine," said I, "it will be done." "Now," I said "I have your mother's ring and I would like to return it."

I reached across the desk and gave it to the oldest daughter. Not a split second later, the younger daughter was out of her chair and lunging for her sister. The husband in the middle was knocked over backwards, hitting his head on the wall and landing on the floor, and the two good looking sisters proceeded to really go at it on the floor.

It was a catfight in the funeral home. WOW!

They were going at it hot and heavy, yelling and screaming. "Mom gave that to me!"

"No, she didn't, she gave it to me!"

"Fuck you! It's mine!"

"Fuck you, no its not!" was heard throughout the serene halls and offices of the funeral home.

This was great stuff.

The two husbands eventually were able to break them apart, and it only lasted a few minutes, but one lady had her dress ripped and the other had a cut lip. And both of them had their hair all messed up.

This was exciting! It was my first, and alas, only catfight I've had the pleasure to witness in a funeral home.

After the husbands pulled their wives apart I, being the perfect undertaker, asked if anybody would like some coffee, and excused myself to go tell my buddies what had just happened, and get the coffee, of course. All the boys walked by slowly, with dignity, and looked discreetly through the glass door. When I came back in with the coffee, the ladies were brushing their hair, and straightening out their clothes. They started apologizing all over themselves to me. I said, "No problem, sometimes anger is the best release for emotions." Or some soft, comforting words like that.

You know us Libras. We're always trying to keep the scales of the world in balance.

The older sister got the ring back; the younger, nothing, and they left the funeral home with torn dresses and a story to tell their grandkids if they dared.

Talk About Money

Another time, a family drove up into the funeral home parking lot in two new Lincolns. I remembered that because we had windows, and I liked Lincolns.

Well, in walks this family, the ladies are wearing furs and diamonds and the men, very expensive suits. There were about 8 of them, and they were here to make arrangements for their father. They wanted direct cremation, no services. Okay, no problem. The less they want, the less I have to do. I got the necessary information for the death certificate and had them sign the cremation consent forms and then we were ready to discuss the obituary.

We wrote up a nice long obituary for this fellow. He had been the president of some big important company. He had probably started there as a kid sweeping the floor, had probably married his high school sweetheart, and had, no doubt, served honorably in the war. After the war he returned to his hometown and together they raised 4 fine college-educated children. And he and his wife had enjoyed traveling the world several times. It was a very nice, long obituary.

When everything was said and done, I asked how the payment for these services was to be handled. "Why," they said, "He's on welfare, state assistance or something like that. He hasn't any money."

So, as I am supposed to do in these unfortunate times of grief and no money, I got out the forms to apply for state assistance, and had them sign them. They drove comfortably away in their new cars, and I submitted the forms to the state.

And, yes, the state, (you and me) paid for this man's service.

I'm not saying that's wrong. But is that right?

A lot of things went on in the funeral home parking lot over the years.

One time a man and a woman pulled into the lot. We were watching them, waiting for them to come inside. They stayed in the car talking a while, and then the woman disappeared from sight. Well, we knew right away what was going on and we all ran to the upstairs windows to get a better view of the peep show going on, outside. By the time we made it upstairs and looked out, the man was leaning back in the seat, and the girl's head was bouncing up and down in his lap. They finished getting to know each other soon enough, and drove away, leaving us with the tissues she had thrown out the car window.

Another time a friend of mine skidded to a stop in the parking lot driving a brand new Kenworth tractor. She had just graduated from Truck Driving School, had a job, a new truck, and was leaving for new horizons. It was nearly quitting time and all the boys went out to check out her new rig. I jumped in and we went out for coffee. Cruising downtown in a big city in big truck is big fun.

Obituaries

When it comes to writing an obituary for the whole world to read, a lot of nice things usually get written about the dead person. How wonderful a fellow he was, and how much he loved and cared for his family and his career, this kind of stuff.

The obituary is the second to the last place where you can have your say, and tell what you want about the person. The funeral is the last place.

You can write whatever you want to in an obit, but usually in most urban newspapers, space is money, so if you want to have your story written, it's going to cost ya.

All undertakers are used to helping people write and place obituaries. That is a part of our job. People nowadays live in several cites over their lifetimes. They die in Hooter Ville, and we have to place an obituary in the newspapers in Beverly Hills, Pixie, Mount Pilot, and New York City. And we do.

Obituaries provide a little advertising for us as well, as you will usually find our name at the bottom. But, more importantly than that, each obituary in the paper lets undertakers know immediately what and how the other undertakers are doing, business-wise. Believe me; the small town undertaker keeps a record of how many dead people the other guy gets. And vice versa. And that can, has, and will forever, lead to the many feuds between competing funeral homes.

One other funny thing that occurs with obituaries and undertakers is this: Say you bury Mr. John Doe. And you never get paid. 2 years later, you read in the morning paper, that your competitor is going to bury Mrs. Jane Doe. Well, now you know the rest of the story. He won't get paid either.

We usually list obituary charges with the other items we call cash advances. This means for the family we pay for these services, on their behalf, whether or not the family pays us.

I had a dirty, stinky drunk fellow bounce in with an obituary he had scribbled for his mother. He wanted us to put it in the paper for him. Tomorrow. I ask to see it. He pulls out of his back pocket a crumpled three page obit. It was scratched up and scrambled, had several beer bottle rings, and had lines crossed out and eraser marks all over the place. His handwriting looked like chicken scratches and I couldn't make heads or tails of what was written.

I ask him if he wouldn't mind rewriting it with my help, but he said no. I called up the paper and asked how much a three-page obit would cost and I was told $1500.00 to $2000.00. I said that the funeral home couldn't submit an obit of that length, written as it was, and accept the charges unless he paid up front. Would that be possible? Well, no, he said. I suggested that he go home and call the obituary into the paper himself and have the paper bill him direct. Which he did. The next day, however, only a very brief announcement was made about his mother.

I read the obits in the paper every day. Many people do. I explain to my families that an obit is primarily a personal announcement of the death of a person. It's not required by law. The county will list the names of the people who died as public record, sometime later, in the paper. Many people have gone this route and have had nothing placed in the papers. I don't agree to this, as putting nothing in the paper will mean nobody will know. This will mean that four weeks from now and forever, people will be coming up to you on the street and asking, "How's old Tom doing?" Then you're left to explain that he died a month ago, and relive all the wonderful events to this person about his death.

Everybody should have a little something said about them. Long or short, that's the point.

Therefore an obit is a very personal article. I explain it as a written chronicle about the person. It may take hours to write one that includes or excludes what you want to be public. Families have had many arguments in my office over the years about writing obits.

Some like a flowery obit, full of love, honey, and sweetness. Others want a point blank, direct notice; like: Joe lived, and now Joe's dead, come to the funeral, the end. It really doesn't matter to me. I prefer the short notices, as I usually have to type them up and fax them off.

The shorter the notice, the less time it takes me, and the less chance of me fucking it up. The notices I hate to type are the ones with the names of all 9 children, 23 grandchildren, 6 great-grandchildren, 3 great great-grandchildren, 6 pallbearers, 8 honorary pallbearers, plus the uncles and aunts and cousins. The next morning, when that paper hits the street, sure as hell somebody's name is going to be spelled wrong, which will be my fault. When that happens, the funeral home (me) will fix the error(s), and re-run the corrected obituary in all the papers. We MAY then charge you the costs of the corrected obituaries; after all, they are corrected. If, however, you bitch and moan about the undue stress the blatantly misspelled name of your dear old great Aunt Daisy which is clearly spelled with an "I" and not a "Y" has caused you and her, we will usually fold and eat all the obituary charges. If the family requested five papers, that's five papers we will be paying for. I used to make many mistakes. Over the years, I have wised up. I suggest that the best way to avoid the undertaker and the newspaper from fucking your obit up, is to bring to the funeral home the obituary typed, edited, spell checked and ready to be faxed. All I have to do is add our name, for recognition, solicitation and prosperity at the bottom and hope.

Them Bones

Funeral homes usually have more dead people in the place, at any given time, than alive. Most have a collection of urns full of dead folks, waiting, like a book on a shelf, to be claimed. These urns are kept in closets somewhere around the place.

We had thousands. People came in every day to claim one and as we would send out four or five urns, we would put six more on the shelf. Every once in a while someone would walk in and say, "Ya know, Granddad was cremated here sometime in 1957or 1958 maybe even 1956, but we don't think anybody ever picked up his urn. Could you check for us?"

Sure enough, we would go to the record book, find the man's name, go to the shelf, and find him sitting there in his urn. We would dust it off, and hand it to the family. The families would be stunned and thankful. I was amazed when we found someone for someone who thought they were lost. I thought that was cool.

One time two ladies came in to claim their mother's urn. She had died some 15 years ago. I went to the records, found her name and, low and behold, also found out that we, the funeral home, had buried this unclaimed urn, along with 500 like it, three or four years before.

Funeral homes are entitled to do this, by law, only after they have sent official notices several times to the family and have waited for two or more years. I checked the records and well, sure as hell, we had buried 500 urns all in a cheap casket a few years back. We had over 2800 in inventory, and we were running out of places to store them. 2800 urns take up a lot of space.

I found in the file the certified letters, envelopes, and copies that showed that we had sent them several notifications of our intent. We had not received any response. Plus we had kept the urn for some 15 years! I was told to explain this to the family.

I went back into the office, file in hand, stepping very gingerly, and as best as I could explained what had happened.

Jesus, Christ! You would have thought the roof was caving in! They both started crying and blubbering that we were terrible, horrible creatures! How could we do such a thing? And so on and so forth they went. I sat there quietly, listening, taking it all in and letting it appear that I was very sympathetic.

Death IS serious, so a good undertaker learns to be patient, and let them have their say.

On the one hand I couldn't blame them for being so mad. I would probably have been mad too. But, on the other hand, as I, when I got the chance to and in my most dignified manner, explained to them "Ladies," I said, "Here are two certified envelopes, with the letters, sent by us, to you, at your address, and they were returned from the post office. You refused to sign for them".

I showed them the dates of phone calls we made to them requesting they come and claim their mother's urn, because it was going to be buried. I showed them the letter inside the certified envelopes and had them read it. "We sent you these indicating that we were going to inter these ashes if they were not claimed." I said, "You received these letters didn't you?" "Yes," they said. "Well, why didn't you accept them and respond to us?" I asked. "Well, we were fighting amongst ourselves as to who should pick them up, and what to do with them." they said; "For, 15 years?" I asked. "Well, we were having family problems." they said. "Can't you understand how we feel?" they asked me. "No," I said, "I cannot." "Why not?" they asked. "Because," I said, "I would never have left my mother's urn sit in a funeral home for 15 years."

Well, saying that went over like a fart in church and we ended up digging up the casket with the 500 urns in it. Two things:

One, all the urns in the casket were made of a fiberboard material.

Two, the casket was also made of fiberboard.

This meant that most of the urns in the casket were mush. We did find the one we were looking for and we returned it to the family. I don't think the funeral home ever buried any urns after that.

Hot Muffins

Some people don't ever want to pick up the urn. They will tell you that. Others can't wait until it's ready and want it, just like a muffin, hot and fresh from the oven.

I have handed out more than a few urns that were still warm from the oven. And I watched as the folks absorbed that fresh, warm urn feeling, and they would go, Mmmm.

If I had time, I would put the urn in the freezer. And this is why:

Crematories, after they warm up, operate at around 1500 degrees. The old machines also need several hours to cool down to a reasonable temperature so that when we open the door, we are not turned to toast. We are not supposed to open the door to get inside and sweep out the cremains until the crematory has cooled down to around a hundred degrees or so. Even then, at 120 degrees, it's a hot, sweaty process. Imagine standing in front of a three foot by three foot gaping hole that is bleeding out hot air at 120 degrees or more, while holding onto a ten foot long special metal broom. It takes about five to ten minutes to (completely) sweep out the retort and another ten to twenty to pulverize the cremains and place them into the urn.

If you are doing this hot, the cremains are going to melt the plastic baggie they first go into, before they go into the urn. That could potentially be a problem for the family later on, depending on what method of disposal they choose. If they decide to scatter dear old dad's ashes to the wind, as he was into wind, this is what will happen: they open the urn on the top of a high and windy mountain, say a few well- chosen words, and carefully lift out the plastic bag for the big farewell, and boom, all his cremains fallout from the bottom of the melted bag dusting all the wrong places. Melted BAG? What the Fuck!!!

When you're hot, you're hot.

Some people want to sweep the cremated remains from the crematory, but the law doesn't allow that. You have to be a licensed to do that.

Many years ago, however, I may have allowed a few folks to do it. I have let more people help me slide the dead into the crematory.

I have had little old ladies tell me they keep their husbands urn sitting on the table beside their chair in the living room. One lady kept her husband on the fireplace mantle. They talk to them. Other people tell me that they don't want anything to do with the urn. As each person is right in his or her own mind, either way is right. Either way you want it, that's the way you'll get it.

Evaporation!

One funeral home I worked for used to have its own brand of crematory. It was long before I was even a twinkle in my father's eye, but it seemed that the owner was an inventor, and he had invented a new, super-duper, first-class, deluxe, toast them, NO toss them, oil-burning crematory.

This crematory evaporated the body. I.e., No Bones' No Ashes (metals excluded). None whatsoever. You were gone! Evaporated! Who would have thought that was possible?!

WOW! That was cool! This crematory energized you to your next location. One minute you are here, and the next, evaporated. Poof!

Whether or not you were blown out of the chimney and scattered all over the neighborhood, I don't know. It was only in use a few years, and then it was replaced by something better. Every once in a while someone would come in, and ask for so and so's urn, who died during that time period, and I would look up in the old records and find out the person had been evaporated. I would explain that to the family, by singing this little melody:

Ashes to Ashes,
Dust to Dust,
Not with us,

That should have been his business motto. Maybe it was.

I have the plaque from the door of this Crematory. I have it hanging in my bar.

Nowadays almost all crematories cook your ass with gas, and you get the ashes. However, new ideas on how better to cook you are popping up, so stay tuned.

Ashes to Ashes, Dust to Dust

Ashes, now that's a misnomer if I ever heard one for cremated remains. I think some undertaker, having just cleaned out his fireplace, started using that word and it just spread around within the industry. It is a softer word than, saying; here are the crushed up bones of Old Joe. Now, almost everybody thinks of ashes when they think of what's inside that nice, little, well not so little, box that holds their relative.

Which sounds better to you?

"Here are the ashes of your husband, Mrs. Smith";

"Here are the cremated remains of your husband, Mrs. Smith,"

"Here are the crushed bones of your husband, Mrs. Smith".

"Here is your husband, Mrs. Smith" Or,

"Here is the urn, Mrs. Smith."

If you picked the last one, you're right. That's what I say to people anyway.

Little do (maybe they don't want to) people realize that what is in that urn isn't ashes; it's the BONES OF THE DEAD.

Ashes come from burned wood or paper. Ashes are light and fluffy when dry. Cremated remains are pulverized bones from the person. They are pulverized down into a kind of flour-type of substance using a heavy duty type of blender. They are not light or fluffy.

People would be amazed at how much an urn would weigh.

Well, your father was a big man, wasn't he???

You are about a 90% water based animal. Take away 90% of your weight, and that will be how much your cremated remains will weigh, give or take a little.

Each person individually gets placed into the crematory and afterwards, all their cremated remains are swept out and pulverized. They must be pulverized. It is a law. Why, you ask? Smaller bones look better than large bones.

In the old days, when cremation was frowned upon by the industry, not used much by society, and regarded as the cheap way out, funeral homes operated within the guidelines of a very few laws regulating cremation. It was very simple. Just burn them and box them, bake them and shake them or toast them and toss them.

Before regulations dealing with the good, bad, and ugly aspects concerning cremation and what to do about the size and how to pulverize the bones, some funeral homes would give the family a box with great big complete leg bones or skull bones in it. 'Well, here's your mother; look, see what a lovely pelvis she has?'

Leg bones are eight, nine or ten inches long, maybe longer. This required big boxes and nice big boxes cost money. They're called urns. You can buy big urns or small urns. I don't know what the hell they used in the old days, but shoe boxes come to mind. They would have worked.

Personally I don't think people would like seeing, when they were opening the box to scatter the contents, the partially identifiable skeleton of their mother. I don't know of any funeral homes that did this, but I have heard stories that this has happened.

I heard a story once about a family who was having a service and was going to scatter the cremated remains. The family opened up the urn, and dug around in the cremated remains looking for another urn. When they realized there wasn't another urn, and that they now had bits and pieces of dear old Johnnie under their fingernails, they sued the funeral home.

One funeral home I worked at used an industrial meat grinder to pulverize the bones. It worked really well, as I have mentioned. The only problem with it was the dust it would make. I would come to work in the morning and there would be twelve pans of bones to grind up. One by one I would push bones into the grinder and out the other end came the pieces. Each pan of bones took a while to run through the machine. When I was finished, there would be a cloud of dust around me that could easily match Pig Pen's. I would have to dust the dust of Cain and Able, George, Betsy, and company, from my hair, and my suit and shoes, before I could go back upstairs.

One time I forgot to do this, and the family noticed that I was covered in dust. I noticed that they noticed this right off. Before they could say anything, I said, "Yes sir, there is a lot of dust that results from pulverizing a skeleton created out of mostly calcium, which is a mineral, like a rock, into cremated remains." I also said: "It's very unhealthy to breathe," which gave the family some satisfaction, and they left without yelling at me.

Another funeral home I worked for used a big tapper to crush the bones. Unfuckingbelievable.
I would have to stand, balancing on a big pan full of bones and smash them into little pieces holding this long handled, and heavy, homemade tool. It had a weighted flat square bottom, like a big stamp. It didn't work too well, as it took a hell of a lot of smashing. The best way was to smash them in small quantities, and then put them all together at the end, so that's what I did. It's a wonder I didn't fall off the pan. If someone had looked through window and seen me, it might have looked like I was churning cream into butter.

With modern technology, now almost all funeral homes have special, high dollar machines that do the pulverizing for us. The new machines turn bone into powder. Powder so fine, you might mistake it for flour or cement. But don't. Many funeral homes even have fans to help to reduce the ash cloud.

Alternatively, how would you like to pick up your mothers urn, a box, with her bones loosely juggling about, and big enough to identify? Well, you could play doctor with them; 'Look, here, here's mother's femur. Can you tell me what this bone is?'

I also never did like the sound of bones shuffling around inside the urn. We used to always pad the inside of the urn so if you shook it, and many did, daddy wouldn't sound like a box of cereal.

Dead Here, Dead There

Have you ever been to Kunta Hora, in Czech Republic? If you like bones, check out the church there. It's not very far away from Prague.

There is a church there that has a chapel, situated in the basement, dedicated to the deaths of some 40,000 people who died because of a plague hundreds of years ago. Not only is the church dedicated to the deaths of these people, the chapel inside is decorated with their bones.

There are huge chandeliers with 20 skulls, and big crosses made of bones, and chambers full of skeletons. 40,000 skeletons, with the bones all pieced together into wonderful displays. There are skulls everywhere, phalanges (finger/toe bones) holding other phalanges. There are leg bones connected to hip bones and hip bones connected to back bones. There are plaques on walls, and tables covered with bones. The dude who built it must have been possessed. He signed his name with bones.

I had my picture taken with my arm resting on a skull and I sent a few postcards to my undertaker friends. It's an amazing place for morbid people like me.

You can take pictures for a few pennies more than the admission fee. I took several.

If you are into bones and skeletons, you must visit this church. Then, if you are a pagan in your religion and philosophy, you should head east to Vilnius, Lithuania.

Lithuania is supposed to be the last pagan state in Europe to have been converted to Christianity. In Vilnius is a church worth your pagan visit. It's called Saint Peter and Paul's Church. It's just a little way away from the Upper Palace grounds, which is the center of town. The church is built on, allegedly, the cult site of a Lithuanian pagan goddess. Her name was Milda. Inside there are over 2000 stuccoed figures, and the coolest figure of them all is the one on the wall, right inside the front door: Death. Yes, the skeleton of Death, with his scythe in hand, watches over all. I thought it was so cool that Death greets you as you enter and exit this peculiar church that I wanted a picture, but, alas, it was Sunday and church services were in full swing. In the middle of the church, above the crowd hanging from the ceiling is a very big Viking ship. With a dragon head made from gold and crystal, and its sail tight with the winds of life, the ship points away from the alter toward Mr. Death.

Very cool. Next time you're there say hi to Mr. Zappa. God rest his soul.

On Christmas Eve many people in Lithuania leave a plate of food for the dead.

Stories About Us

There are a lot of stories going around about funeral homes. We are an unusual but necessary component of any society. Here is another one. Everybody knows you can return a new pair of shoes; but what if you were the store, the shoes were your dead dad, and the funeral director brought back your dad? Well, there is one story about an owner of a funeral home who did do just that.

This story made its way into a trade journal. The family would not pay the bill or sign some papers or something, and so the undertaker brought old Joe back and sat him down on the front steps of the family home.

I hope the undertaker at least dressed the dead guy in street clothes so it would give the impression to the neighbors that Old Joe hadn't really died; he had just gone away and now, he was back. If, I'd been that stupid and had done something stupid like that, I would have gone the whole ten yards. I'd have put a knife in one hand and a piece of wood in the other and made him look like he was whittling on a stick.

This went over real well, and the undertaker, now, is probably not one. I'd bet you Old Joe was laughing all the way.

Be Still, My Love

When people would come in and ask for Mr. So and So's urn; we would ask if he was a big man. If the answer was yes, we would then go and fill an urn with a little more ashes. If the answer was no, then they would get a little less.

This never happened, I swear, but it was a joke we would tell our friends.

There have been many of the same stories about sex and the dead told and retold to me over the years. All these sick stories are sick if you ask me. And, I'm a sick fuck, but I will say this.

I have only seen, one dead, stunningly beautiful woman. Only one, who could have made me a member in that; Hush, Hush, I love the cool touch, secret society of Necrophilacs.

The woman was in her twenties, and she looked beautiful dead. This is after seeing hundreds of dead women. This girl had been autopsied; she had a zipper from her snatch to her tits, with another one around her head to boot.

The boys at the M.E.'s rolled the table out with her on it and threw off the sheet then they started kidding the kid, (me) saying; "You can have a go, if ya want. You better have a go, be quick before it's too late." No one did. We took care of this poor girl and nobody touched her.

You read about it happening and see it in the movies. I know of no one personally who would ever, and has, ever done that, except;

I did hear of a story involving a woman undertaker and a dead guy once. It was in all the trade journals, if you read this story before, read it again.

This undertaker had left the place with this old boy in the back. He was going get lucky one more time. She must have done it a time or two. She was caught and lost her license and who knows or cares what happened to her. I want to know what happened to the guy. Did it take three hours and two undertakers to get the smile off his face?? When I read this story I lived in an apartment building and a neighbor friend of mine had lived in the same town where it had happened. She confirmed what I had read from her hometown papers.

You might be wondering how??? You can embalm a penis and make it stiff as a rock. I've seen it done more than once, and she undoubtedly had, too. But, why?

You know why.

This puts a whole new meaning to a being a dead lay.

Ya know being an undertaker has another great (sic) plus: you get to see your friends naked. I know some girls have hang-ups about that and don't want to be seen dead and naked; thinking they will be leered over by a male undertaker, friend or stranger. For you guys out there with the big dicks, I might measure you out. If you don't want to die and be goggled at because you are the finest looking lady in town, find a lady embalmer, or be cremated.

We get to see all the ugly of dead nakedness too, my friend. Believe me, most of us are plain ugly.
I have a black T-shirt with NECROCLUB on the front of it. On the back is a picture of a dead woman with big tits lying on a table covered with a sheet. Above her it says: Be Still My Love. I only wear the shirt on special occasions, like the Festival of the Dead Parade. This is a day celebrated in Mexico, and in my state, once a year. I am not a member of any club. I prefer warm and jumpy girls to cold and stiff ones.

Milk Moustache

Yes, there are magazines for undertakers too.

My grandfather used to collect barbed wire, and there were magazines for that.

I wonder if there are magazines for under-water basket-weaving.

Trade magazines for undertakers are there to remind us about the joys and wonders of being an undertaker. They also remind us about the seriousness of our profession. 'Death is Serious' they proclaim. They also explain in detail all the new techniques that have been devised to fix up the dead, and make them look like they're not dead. Some ideas are quite good; others don't work so well. There was an article once about using milk to embalm bodies. It makes your bodies as smooth as milk. It didn't go over well.

Had it worked, the dairy industry, hand in hand with the embalmers of the world, could have made millions. All we needed to do was put milk moustaches on dead celebrities. Somehow, I don't think the dairy business would want a milk moustache campaign using dead celebrities. The dead celebrities probably would, though, for the royalties and continued publicity.

Some articles in our trade journals seem to think undertakers have nothing else to do and have easily twenty-plus hours to work on a body. Sometimes, you do. Sometimes it takes three to four hours to embalm and sew up an autopsied corpse. If the dead dude had a smashed-in face full of the windshield he was stuck to, and mom wants to give her son a goodbye kiss, you are going to need three or four more hours plus or minus to make that mess look like a face. Often you also have several other bodies to prepare, and don't have the five hours at that time to spare. If, however the family still requested a viewing, after being informed of the conditions in the politest of ways, off I would go into the land of needles and thread. Sometimes, when I got the blood and guts all cleaned up, the damage to the skin around the face isn't so bad, and with a little bit of magic they are looking GOOD.

Other times ten tons of putty couldn't put Humpty Dumpty together again. I can make dead look dead, but it takes a trick unbeknownst to me to make the dead look alive.

I still read the trade journals from time to time and have picked up a few tricks. You can buy from these trade magazines a putter shaped like a casket.

One time, I had just started a job in a little town. It was my first Friday night and I found myself sitting home reading an undertaker's magazine. "Fuck this shit!"

I couldn't believe myself. I put the phones on the service, grabbed a pager, and left the place running, and quickly road my Harley to a bar.

The Body Shop

We get people in all the time with their heads torn off or their faces ripped to pieces; bodies with arms and legs missing, and some with parts of the torso torn off. We also get bodies burnt into crispy critters.

And, of course, it's these people that the family wants to see. "Thank God we only have to make the face and hands viewable," an old timer told me once. I have spent a few long nights sewing a head back into shape. I have spent hours re-creating, using wax and cosmetics, the eye or the lips of the mouth, so that it (kind of) looks right. That's right, it kind of looks right. Sometimes when there was no hope for a facial viewing we would show only the hands, or one hand. Show them something for them to touch, and see. We would cover the head and seal it inside a plastic bag, which was tied at the neck. Then we would cover that with a soft clean sheet. Most of the time we were congratulated on our efforts, whatever we did, and the families would be very touched. Other times you spent 15 hours just for someone to come in, take a 20 second look, and say, 'Well, he looks terrible'. Told ya.

I heard a story about an undertaker, who, after being told that the dead fellow didn't look like himself, said to the family, "Well, you've never seen him dead before have you?"

The flip side is that sometimes they look so good dead you don't have to do anything. You die without any injury, peacefully in your sleep; a healthy young professional on your way up, and you'll look just as good, dead.

Do you really want to see your mom with a different nose, this one made out of wax, maybe leaning a bit to the left, and make believe Kaleidoscope eyes with 2 inches of stitches forming a faint track down her face?

Of course you do. But remember my friend, that face will likely be covered with layers of makeup, which is then powdered over thick and thin. If you give her a kiss, your lips are going to look like you just ate a powdered donut.

That looks good when it's done at the end of the funeral and the person coughs, and has to wipe off their face in front of everybody.

Or, would you like to remember her the way she was before she died?

Some people have to say goodbye in person. Some don't. It all comes down to choice.

It's my job to do what is asked of me, and I do it. But I'm the first one to explain the seriousness of the injuries to the family right up front. I also explain to them that there isn't any way possible for me to correct the extent of the damage and attempt to recreate a natural appearance. If the heads half gone, it is half gone. You find the other half, and I'll sew it back on.

Funeral homes have all kinds of ways to make the good, bad and ugly look better. We use colored shawls and drape them over the casket, which (kind of) hides things. We use soft, red light bulbs in the lamps. And we have every kind of makeup known to man to repair and conceal the damage. From fingernail polish to cavity filling putty, we have it all.

This old man used to say, "Dim the lights, speed up the music, they'll never see it through the tears."

Boy, there is truth in that.

Hell, we're not a body shop. We're THE body shop! You run your head through a brick wall, and we fix you up with putty, paint and powder. You won't look like you, but you won't care, will you?

I picked up a young girl who had been at the wrong place at the wrong time. She was killed when the motorcycle she was a passenger on hit a truck. Most of the upper part of her head above the eyebrows was missing. Other than a few scrapes and cuts, and the fact she was separated from her left leg, that was all the damage. Her parents wanted to see her. I wrapped her head with a new white towel, just above the eyes which made it appear like she had just washed her hair, secured the towel, and covered her body with a sheet and a blanket. Then I let the family say goodbye.

They needed to say goodbye.

I have spent the entire night working on someone, getting them ready for a viewing, only to get a phone call the next morning. No, we don't want to see him. We've changed our minds. Oh, well.

We had a woman want to see her boyfriend once. He had been beheaded in some kind of accident.

She knew that, of course, but still wanted to say goodbye to him in person. So, my buddy and I went to work. We washed and dried his head and neck so that they could be kissable. Then we did the same for his shoulders. We slid him onto a viewing table, wrapped him in a plastic sheet, and set his head and what was left of his neck, on his shoulders. We used a clean white towel and wrapped it tightly around his neck. Finally, we covered him up with sheets, a pillow, and blankets, and rolled him into the chapel.

She thought he looked great.

Black Cars

When I was a kid in the business I used to like to drive the limousines. The hearses too, but in the limos you looked important. In the hearses you looked just like an undertaker.

I was riding in a brand new black six door Buick once with a co-worker, a little older than me, at the wheel. We were coming back from having dropped off the family or, maybe we dropped off some flowers. I don't know why I was riding with him. Anyway, he said, "Watch this" and he hit the emergency brake, as we took a hard, fast, right turn from one busy street, onto another semi-busy street. Boy! That big black six door Buick slid almost half way around in the street. And we came to a stop facing the wrong direction. The driver's side hubcap popped off, and went rolling down the street until it hit a parked car and stopped. There we were, sitting in a brand new 6-door funeral limo, in the street, facing the wrong direction, blocking traffic and the car wouldn't start. The light had changed and now cars were stopped in front of us. The car was flooded, and as he tried desperately to get it started, I jumped out and got the hubcap. He got the car started, we turned around, and away we went. Scared shitless! We drove into an alley and I put the hubcap back on. He drove carefully after that, just like limo drivers are supposed to, back to the funeral home. We both feared that we would soon be called into the boss' office and fired, because we figured someone would call and complain. After all, there was only one six-door limo in town. Luckily, nothing ever happened.

I went on a house call, in my youth, with a partner. He was more experienced with the families so he went inside and made the arrangements. I sat outside in the black station wagon, which I had parked on the side the road.

After a while, my partner walked out and asked me to back the car down the driveway beside the house

"Okay. No problem." I said. I was cool; I could back anything up, anywhere. And, just because there happened to be a bunch of kids milling about, all of whom were checking out the black hearse, and wondering who died up in that old house: the grumpy old man or the nice old lady who made cookies, I didn't even turn my head. I just used the mirrors. I backed that car right down into a deep ditch. The kids laughed their heads off at me.

We had to get the wrecker to pull it out. After that, he drove us away.

To Tint or Not to Tint

For a little while we used a fucking Pinto station wagon to haul bodies in. Can you believe it? To make the cot fit, the passenger seat back had to be right against the dashboard. When you were loaded, and driving back to the funeral home, you could rest your arm on the person's foot or head, depending on which way you had them on the cot. We had the windows tinted. Nobody liked driving in that cheap, weak, rattle-ass tin death trap, and it went away.

Another funeral home I started with used a station wagon to make removals with and they didn't tint the windows. Jesus Christ. That was stupid. I got that fixed.

There was a story about an undertaker who had driven into a town from far away to pick up a dead fellow and transport him back to his promised land. Well, it seems that after picking up the body, this undertaker fellow decided to check out some of the city's finest ladies dancing naked and have a few beers in a strip club, which was right smack DOWN TOWN. The headlines in the next day's papers said it eloquently; 'Body in car,

Undertaker in bar.' This dumb fuck parked his black funeral car on main street; mistake number one; mistake number two was he left the dead guy's foot uncovered, and hanging out there for the world to see, and, well, guess what..? Someone saw it. He went to jail, and someone else had to drive over and bring that fellow home.

Off the Grid

People live and die in the most out of the way places. I have driven up some harrowing roads to some God-forbidden, piece of shit shack in the woods more than several times. Houses kind of like Ma and Pa Kettle had: with chickens, pigs and goats running around, not a speck of paint, and dogs trying to tear my leg off. Many of the houses were half-built with wrecked cars out front, and a yard full of weeds. It's usually early in the morning, more often than late in the day. It's someone who lived alone, and usually, had been dead there a LONG, LONG, time. A neighbor had been wondering about old So and So, and came up. If they had not been found for a few more weeks only a skeleton would remain. That's much easier to pick up than what you usually find.

Justice

It's sad the way some people have to die.

I went on a call to the Medical Examiner's office to pick up 3 women: 2 ladies and a 12 year old girl.

I didn't go to the scene; the cops and the coroners saw that. Each woman was stabbed about 60 times. Everywhere! He had really cut them up. It made me sick.

The boys who did told me it was a bloodbath. I couldn't believe a human could do that to another human.

The guy who did it had been sent to prison for raping one of these women, I think. He had somehow escaped from prison, and had tracked her down along with her friend and daughter at home one morning.

The cops caught him, not long afterwards, and they fried his ass at the state prison. Goodbye.

Motherfucker and God Bless Capitol Punishment.

I got lucky and fried a murderer once.

He too had killed a couple of women. He was found guilty, and had been in jail for years, appealing on the grounds that capitol punishment was too severe. He lost. When it came time to walk that green mile, as it was called in a movie, he went crying and shaking, and had to be practically carried all the way to the injection room. Later, along with a police escort, he came to me. The cops were happy. One shook the dead guys hand right before we shoved him in. I felt good pushing the button. "See ya Asshole."

Guys almost always blow their head off when they kill themselves. It's much easier on us when women do it. They usually take a bunch of pills.

I once worked in a funeral home that sat way below, and to the side, of a long tall bridge. The bridge spans a lake, several roads, houses and businesses. You could look up and make out people walking across. One time I saw a person standing on the outside of the railing. There were police and fire trucks and their lights were what caught the attention of someone in our office. So, we all watched. They saved that person. Some of the boys who worked there had said they had seen a person jump. A small percentage of the jumpers would actually survive the fall, which was several hundred feet. A larger percentage would not. Some of them would wash up, right near our back door. We would hear the coroners yelling and go check it out. Quite convenient, wouldn't you say?

There is a subconscious feeling about bridge jumping suicide seekers. I think some think they will survive jumping, if they land in the water. And some do. They survive with massive internal injuries and multiple broken bones and most grow old a paraplegic. The jumpers who are serious, aim for and bounce off the ground.

I got a kid who killed himself and two other people using his car. He was attempting to make it look like an accident. He was trying to hit the other cars head on, which were traveling in the other direction. Several had avoided him, and someone had called the cops, who were trying to catch him. He had traveled about 20 miles until he hit and killed two nice old folks.

What a shitty thing to do. Don't kill somebody else for fucking up your own fucked up life.

I heard a story on a late night T.V. show about a guy who, before he fell over dead, shot himself either five or six times with a single shot rifle. It must have been a twenty-two rifle. After each bullet lodged itself somewhere inside him, the guy would have to reload the rifle, cock it, point it at himself, and use something to pull the trigger. Bang! Bang! "Gee, ain't I dead yet?" Bang! Bang! Bang! "What the hell?" Bang!

I'm an undertaker. I can believe it.

One Day in the Life of an Undertaker

I have to go to the hospital. There is a baby boy there. The mother is holding her new son when I enter the room. She's crying. I stood there almost an hour before I said a word. What could I say? She didn't want to let go and I couldn't blame her. It was almost another hour before she gave me her son.

Ever Been to a Hanging?

Have you ever been to a hanging? I have been to several.

There is a neat trick to moving a dead body, hanging, if you're lucky enough to get there in time. You lift up the guy's legs and roll the cot under him, and then you untie the rope. Easy, Peasy, just like tying your shoe. A good hanging is just about the easiest pickup I have ever made.

At one hanging, in a house on a hill, during the dead of winter, in the middle of a foggy night a long ways from anywhere, I slipped and fell down the outside stairs and cracked a couple of ribs. Damn, that hurt for months. I had to have the coroner move the cot into place. And do all the heavy work for me. The cabin was complete with several empty bottles of booze and lots of trash that had not made it to a trash can.

I went to another hanging where the hung had shot himself to boot. He had it all set up. He had the rope tied to a sign in a campground, along with a stool, and a gun. He shot himself, and then kicked away the stool. I guess he wanted to make sure he got the job done right, and he did.

The best hanging I went to, I didn't see. The boys from the coroner's had already cut this young boy down. He was lying on the carpet when I got there. He was found hanging in a closet naked, with all the good kinds of kinky shit sticking in and out of him. He came and went, or cum and gone as they say. Before he was found he had a few days to hang around. There are some sexual freaks out there.

I picked up a dead guy who had bled to death by ripping a hole in his rectum from using a potato masher in there. Maybe he did have a potato in there, I didn't look.

One Man Show

I knew an undertaker once who used to go to homes of the dead, all the time, alone. He was a one man show. He was the only one I knew at the time who did that. I guess he would ask the family if there was any assistance at the home, and if there was, he would get them to pick up the body, put it on the cot and, help him take it to the car. He told me, "It's the least they can do."

I worked funerals for him when he needed help with a really big show. One time when I was a kid at a funeral in his place he came up to me and moved the pen over in my shirt pocket so that it was behind my suit jacket and out of sight. I have never forgotten that, and to this day, I do not expose the pen while wearing a suit jacket. TABOO.

I was told this fellow would also go to nursing homes alone and if they had stairs, and believe me, most STILL have stairs, and if he couldn't find help he would slid the bodies down the stairs and then put them on the cot.

I have used his method of having the family do the heavy lifting in homes myself, when there was assistance. Not too many sons or daughters are going to refuse to help carry their mother.

My back thanks them.

A lot of undertakers have bad backs. However, just being an undertaker for the most part is really a lazy job. We sit at a desk and type. We sit and listen and talk to people. We move caskets around, and we stand around looking sharp at funerals, and we get to drive the hearses. To the lay person, that's just about it. That is, until the phone rings at 0, 3 hundred, and we have to go. Off again on a safari hunt to find, lift, and return with what could be a 300-pound dead woman or an 80-pound dead man. It usually doesn't work out the way I want.

This is America, the fattest of the fattest, and I'm right there with the rest. I used to correlate my weight swings with the death rate. When the death rate was slow, I had time to get some exercise, and I wouldn't, so I got fat. When the whole world was dropping dead to see me, the few minutes of actual lifting I did couldn't compete with the lifting of cheeseburgers and fries. I feel sorry for the poor undertaker who gets to lift my dead ass off the floor. Maybe I'll hide inside a car in a garage and make it fun.

You Only Bury Your Friends

If you are a small-town undertaker employee, working for a funeral home, and it's just you and the owner, you will have plenty to do to keep yourself busy. If there aren't any bodies lying around, the boss might have you painting the chapel, his house, the funeral home or all of the above. If it's nice outside, you might be fertilizing, watering, and mowing the yard or weeding the flowerbeds. You will probably wash the owner's cars. I've done all that. It makes the day go by. If you're leaning, you should be cleaning. Undertakers are like the Maytag repairman. We are always waiting, always waiting for the phone call.

If you are the owner of a funeral home, the waiting can drive you crazy. I know of no one else whose depression ceases, when someone else ceases to exist, than the owner of a funeral home. They are happiest when the preparation room is knee-deep with dead bodies, and everybody else in town is sad. I have never been an owner of a funeral home, thank God. But, bills are bills and funeral homes have bills to pay, just like every other business. When you are the hired help, you must be paid, so the boss must find something for you to do.

Another thing about being a small-town undertaker is this: you must make friends to bury friends. There ain't a small-town undertaker around that can survive on burying his enemies. This is kind of sick in a way. You pass yourself off as genuine and honest, but, really, you have an alternative motive. You know it and they know it. Time passes, however, and you either make it or you don't. If you make it, you are genuine and honest, accepted and respected. You make friends and acquaintances in the town, and then you bury them.

Beg, Borrow or Steal

When we arrive to pick up the dead, inside our cot is supposed to be a crisp, clean, white sheet. We use this to gently wrap the recently departed with. Many times, however, I have, in front of an audience, unfolded the sheet and found a big, dark, red, or brown stain, right in the middle. Fuck! This looks very professional, let me tell ya. If you're lucky, for emergencies like this, you have another sheet hidden away. Then you can apologize and blame it on the laundry service. If you don't have a spare sheet, beg, borrow, or steal one. Do NOT wrap momma in a shit-stained, blood-soaked sheet.

Glass Slippers

One time, I met a family and we arranged a nice funeral for dear old dad. We went to the selection room and the family picked out a nice simple casket. Everything was smooth sailing. The family left and I went downstairs to the cooler, which was what we called the refrigerator, to get this man out and embalm him. Oh Shit! This boy was a big man! I hadn't laid eyes on him, before now. I embalmed him, dressed him in his very tight, Sunday, go-to-church clothes, and went and got the casket. Do you know what a 370 pound, six foot, six inch man looks like inside this simple casket? Damn,   uncomfortable that's what!

When we dropped him in that casket, he looked like a man jammed in a can. We could hardly get him out again. He was stuck tight. His shoulders were all hunched in close to his chest and his elbows were touching his nipples. His legs were too long for the casket, and we had to cut them off--- just kidding. They had to be bent up at the knees, just to fit. The lid to the casket wouldn't fit and close properly, because he was pushing out the sides and bending the hinges of the casket.

Now what the fuck do we do?

Well, casket companies have made arrangements for this situation. We called the warehouse and had an extra-large casket sent over. I had never heard of them before. Extra-large caskets come in sizes marked 1X, 2X, and 3X. Each one is a couple inches longer, and wider. I think we used a 2X for that boy. We had to eat the extra cost of the casket, which was different from the one they had picked out and I had destroyed. I explained the situation to the family when they saw him in a different casket the next day. They understood very well. They had wondered about that same thing.

Death and Children

Children are more aware than most people think when someone has died. All they need is time and understanding to help them get it straight in their heads, and understand what has happened.

I talked to a family one time that included a little boy. He wanted to see his grandpa. I walked them all into the viewing room and showed the little boy his granddad. He was about 7 or 8 years old and was a little handicapped. He asked me all kinds of questions. How come his eyes are closed? And, could he open one of them? I explained about the eye caps we used to keep the eyes closed. He touched his face, and his hands, and he wondered why his granddad was so cold. I explained how a body is only warm when it is alive and breathing, and when it is dead, it is only as warm as the temperature of its surroundings. After asking all these questions, he still had a puzzled look on his face. I asked him if he had any more questions, and he asked "why did you cut his legs off?"

I said we would never do that to his granddad. To prove it to him, I removed the casket spray, and lifted the lower part of the casket so he could have a look. He touched his granddad's legs, and his shoes, and he smiled. His granddad was whole, and not cut in two as he had thought. The family really thanked me for taking the time to answer the boy's questions and to let him see his entire grandpa.

Now is a good time for good undertaker vs. bad undertaker.

The good undertaker would have made sure the dead fellow's shoes were shined and trousers creased, as I had. A bad undertaker might not even have put his shoes on, fuck the shining. Nobody looks under there! I've done that too.

While I was on the Isle of Man, a neat little island between England and Ireland, I had the pleasure of watching a blind little girl explore the feeling of my motorcycle. I had ridden to the Isle of Man to ride the world famous racecourse, and had got lucky and had found a place to stay; for free, if I played my guitar. Later that night, I had walked out from the pub/hotel to go for a ride. As I jumped on and warmed up my motorcycle I noticed a little girl about seven years old, pulling her mom toward my bike. I could tell then that this little girl was blind. I turned off my bike and started talking to her. She wanted to touch the bike, so I led her to the right front, and she touched everything with her fingers on that side of the bike. Nothing was hot yet, so she didn't get burned. She walked around and spun the back wheel, and ran her fingers over everything on the left side. I told her it was a BMW motorcycle. I asked her if she wanted to sit on it. 'Yeah, yeah', she said. With her mother's approval, I picked her up and sat her on it and put her hands on the handlebars. Do you want to start it and hear it run? 'Yeah, yeah' she said, so I let her. She really liked the sound and the feel of the bike, and she revved it up several times. I asked her mom if she wouldn't mind if I took her for a little ride, but she didn't think it was a good idea. It was just starting to rain at the time. She got off, said thank you and good-bye. I took off to find another bar. I'm sure that little girl will not forget that, and maybe she will be a motorcycle enthusiast.

I stayed a few nights at that bar. After closing it down the first night the owner, the local constable and I shared a joint. I rode the course 2 times in the rain and never once went over 85 miles an hour. I don't think the boys who race it ever go under 85.

A Cot or Not

Two boys in the middle of a snowy winter were bringing a body out from a house on the cot. The steps were covered with ice, and as one thing leads to another, they slipped, lost hold of the cot, and ass over teakettle, it went, into the flower garden. It landed wheels up, body down. Oops!

A cot can weigh around 100 pounds on its own, including the seat belts. Throw on 200 pounds of dead weight, and MAN! You've really got yourself some load to move around the china shop. Even with 150 pounds of dead meat the cot is tough to lift, turn and carry around the many obstacles that lie between us and our car. If that sucker gets off-balance, over it is going to go. If you're the unlucky fellow in its path, look out! Heads UP!

As unbelievable as it sounds, there is a head end and a foot end to a cot. Usually, it doesn't matter, but on the foot side of the cot there is a bar, just about 6 inches high. You place the feet there and the body will stay put if you have it strapped in tight, and right. Which is what you want the body to do, when you have the cot standing straight up like a hand truck, and you are wheeling it through a narrow trailer, or when you and it are riding in a very small elevator.

Some elevators are not made to haul a cot in. I have stood up many a cot to ride the elevator in an apartment building, condominium, or retirement home. I don't know what the designers were thinking, but they must not think anybody is going to die in their place. Thank God cots are designed to be stood straight up. Oh yeah, thank God for elevators too.

I had an old cot jammed into an elevator once with a body on it. I must have hit the latch which unlocks the legs, because when the elevator doors opened on the basement floor, the head end of the cot collapsed and the body slid out from the cot onto the floor. I couldn't hold the cot up and do anything to stop the body sliding, once the cot dropped. It was very early in the morning, but a nurse saw what happened. I quickly slid the body back onto the cot, lifted it up, and got the hell out of there.

I was sweating the phone call over that fuck up. Thank God it never came.

Hospitals

Hospitals are very busy places for the living and soon not-to-be-living. There are, in the evening, always lots of people coming and going, visiting those who are in worse shape than themselves. One time I had to get someone from a hospital room in a small hospital. It was the middle of the evening. The floor I went to was packed with folks. As I walked out from the elevator into the crowded lobby, pushing my cot, people parted that lobby like I was Moses and I walked down the hall to my room. When I had loaded my luggage and signed all the papers, I had to wade back through the sea of people to the elevator. As I, with my cot now fully loaded, waited for the elevator doors to open and take me away from being the center of attraction in this crowded lobby, up to the elevator walks an entire wedding party.

A fucking wedding party at a hospital! The whole fucking nine yards too; Bride in White, Groom in a tux, both with their family and friends in tow and all decked out. When they saw me and my cot standing there, they did a double take, let me say that!

The bride started crying, the groom started yelling. The conversations around the lobby stopped, people stared, and the world stood still for a few seconds. I stood there until the doors opened, got inside and split.

Nobody wants to share a ride in an elevator with an undertaker and his dead body. Very few people, anyway. Over the years, I have had more people stand back and let me enjoy the ride alone, than come along. Those that do are always anxiously waiting for the elevator doors to open.

After the doors close a strange, short-lived, kind of intimate relationship develops between me, my dead body, and the person sharing the ride. Many have asked me, "who is it?" Others have asked who it is. More than you think have asked me, "What's on that cot?"

When the elevator doors open they practically run out. I have always wanted to have a fake hand on a stick, so that I could reach under the cot and touch someone in an elevator with it.

The reaction you get from the folks waiting to get in the elevator and see me walk out when the doors open is the same. They stop talking and part the waters so I may walk by.

My partner and I went to a shit hole apartment on the 4th floor, in a piece of shit building, and picked up a dead piece of shit who was lying in his own shit! (You've got to love your job, you know.)

This apartment building didn't have an elevator, so we had to carry the cot four floors up an outside set of rickety stairs. The stairs consisted of rotten boards for handrails, nails sticking out and it was missing some steps. The building was also in the wrong part of town, if you know what I mean.

Out in the hall we scoped out the scene. The cops, the medical examiners and we noticed the three or four guys who were hanging around, watching us from the outside hallway on the other side of the building. We went inside the apartment. All there was in the place was a bed, a radio, an old TV set, and a dead guy. We got the body on the cot and slowly made our way back down the rickety stairs and left. I'll bet a hundred dollars that that apartment was not empty five minutes before the TV and the radio were gone.

Johnny on the Spot

Almost all big city hospitals have a morgue where the body is taken and metaphorically speaking, stored on ice. In reality, as on T.V., they are not kept on ice. In due time, we, the smoother movers, will arrive.

They use special tables in hospitals to move the dead bodies about. Orderlies, grunts, or hospital staff personnel will come to the room where the body died, and load it onto this secret table. These tables look empty, and are completely draped with a sheet which goes to the floor. The body is hidden on a shelf below. These are much more discrete while moving the body around. But, now you know to watch for them.

Morgues are a beautiful thing for the undertaker. We can come and pick up our package without the urgency of most house calls. And, we can come anytime without disturbing the other guests. Hell, we don't even have to dress up.

Several small-town hospitals don't have a morgue. The bodies stay dead on the spot. I, Tombstone Todd the Undertaker, have to drive up, park right next to the front door, walk right through the front door strolling and rolling my cot across the lobby to the front desk, for introductions. After that, I have to work right next to or beside families who have loved ones dying in the bed next to the one I want. It's not a time to tell jokes with the staff. The look in the eyes of some of the patients I've seen looking at me in the I.C.U. wards who were dying was freaky. These people aren't dead, yet. I'll be back and they know it. I get to walk by them twice: once empty, and once loaded. That must be a Kodak moment for them.

Picture this: Here you are in the lobby of the I.C.U. of your local hospital with your family. You're talking softly about granny and how she might not make it, because this is her third operation, and she is, after all, 95 years old. But, she is a tough old girl and we should think positive and pray. Right then, along comes the undertaker, he and his cot as shiny as a new nickel, softly whistling a tune. The sight of this usually stops all conversation dead. I have received looks that could kill from people watching me stroll back and forth.

I went to the same hospital three times in one night. And I met with some of the families that watched me go by earlier.

One guy even asked me, "Say, um, haven't you already been here enough?" "Yes;" I solemnly replied.

In reality, however, the more people die, the more I make! Keep on dying out there!!

The biggest benefit of going to all the hospitals and nursing homes again and again are the girls. I've dated several nurses, having met them picking up the dead. It's a perfect situation. I'm looking sharp and business-like, and they're working. After going to the same hospital or nursing homes twenty times you get to know the staff. The next step is easy. "Would you like to get together for a drink sometime?"

Play Through

I've picked up the dead on a golf course. Hey, why not die playing golf?

He probably got a hole in one, couldn't believe his luck, and didn't have the money to buy the house a round when he got to the clubhouse. We went out and he was whisked away. Everyone on the course just played on through.

I went to the theater once, not to watch the play but to play with the dead.

An old gentleman had died at a fancy theater and the old man and I went to pick him up. His wife asked for his belt, money, wallet, shoes and tie before we could leave the lobby where the paramedics had laid him down. That must have been some play.

I saw Swan Lake, preformed in the Bolshoi Theater in Moscow Russia. It was absolutely UN—fucking believable! Well worth the trip. It brought tears to my eyes, but it didn't kill me.

Money Enough to Die

How much money do you think you will have in your pockets, when you die? 5 bucks? $50 bucks? The most I have ever found and counted out for a family was around $2500.

This guy was going to drink himself to death. And he did. The bartender told my partner and me that he had come into the bar a couple of days ago, and said he was going to drink himself to death. He drank all day and night, from open to close and he didn't eat. He didn't even drink a glass of water. It took him two or three days before he croaked, but he still had that much money left in his wallet.

Gangsters and drug dealers usually have thousands of dollars or more when they're killed. I sure wish I could pick up one of those guys once and find the hidden money. No, just kidding. I don't need that.

I returned a wallet that had some money in it to a family once. After I counted out the money, and handed the wallet to them, I asked for their signature as a receipt for the returned money. They signed the receipt. There was only about fifteen dollars. They opened up the wallet and inside a hidden pocket was a 50-dollar bill. Only they knew about it. Mad money, they said.

That family trusted me.

A Boy Scout is trustworthy, loyal, helpful, friendly, courteous, kind, obedient, cheerful, thrifty, brave, clean, and reverent. I am an Eagle Boy Scout.

I have been blessed as an undertaker. I have had more bodies piss on me than families pissed at me.

Less than 10 families come to mind, and after helping thousands, that isn't too bad. I could be wrong, I admit it. The times when shit really hit the fan, well, most of them were my fault.

Chalk it up to human nature or a difference of personalities. Undertakers aren't perfect.

Sometimes you just get off on the wrong foot.

A family got pissed at me for calling them up and expressing my condolences, and asking if they had any questions. Granted, it was around 3AM or so. But get this:

After a funeral home gets a phone call that we have a body to pick up and we have picked it up and are back at the office, we usually call the family. This is standard practice in many funeral homes. What the hell, the family is usually up anyway. They just got the same call from the same place of death, just like us, only earlier, so it isn't like we just woke them up. Some folks will drive for hours after that call to see old Joe dead in the hospital. Others won't. After the family is called and the coast is clear, look out, here we come.

Our call to the family lets the family know that the body is safe and secure at the funeral home, resting comfortably, and we are awaiting further instructions. Some families instantly have 20 questions to ask us, right then; others don't, but appreciate the call and concern. Some are upset.

This family got mad. They didn't like me calling them up telling them something they already knew. And no, they didn't have any questions. Later that day, the arrangement conference didn't go too well either. During the arrangement conference, I needed to excuse myself and get some more forms. I accidentally slammed a door going from room to room to get them. I had to keep the doors closed so my cat, Fred, would not be let out to jump into momma's lap.

The inconsiderable rudeness of my slamming of those doors, mixed with the differing personalities between the daughter, her mother and me, coupled with the phone call earlier, only helped dig my grave deeper. I just couldn't do anything right with this family to make them happy. To make matters worse, the newspaper managed to really fuck up his obituary. That wasn't my fault this time, but it didn't matter. I had made damn sure that the obituary I had faxed to the paper was correct down to the last letter. I didn't need any more trouble from this family. The newspaper didn't proofread its copy and it came out all wrong. This cemented my grave and I could do no more. I was shit, in shit city, and I stunk.

Shit

I'm used to it.

I have reached my hand under a body more than a few times, but not many, only to come out with a handful of the stinky stuff. I learned soon enough; roll the body, look under the body, then put your hand there and pull the sheet through to the other side.

It's really funny when your partner puts his hand in shit.

I have had shit and piss run down my arms and over my chest when I have carried someone from the bed to the cot. And I ain't shitting.

Some nursing homes are notorious for letting their patients, dead or alive, lie in piss and shit. I hated that.

The old boys called them 'Piss Palaces'! You could smell it from the moment you walked in. I can't blame them for not wanting to do it. It's a shitty job. But, yes, I can blame them. It's part of their job to keep their patients clean.

Maybe, however, because the patient is dead, they can overlook it, or look around it, or just not look at it anymore.

Nursing home helpers should be paid more. Most of them have thankless jobs. They work hard, taking care of people that no one else wants to care for.

It has to be very tough working with people who don't know what the hell is going on anymore. Most of these people can still kick, bite, spit, punch, and yell at you like nobody's business. And many do. I have been grabbed by and yelled at by several little old men and women who didn't know what day it was. They somehow know who the undertaker is.

It's nice to be popular.

You can sense them watching you as you walk down the hall. They all have their eyes on you. Their eyes follow you all the way to the dead person's room and back.

We undertakers usually park around back at nursing homes, if that's an option. Usually near the garbage cans is where you will find us. That way no one knows when we come and go. But when we enter the facility, we usually still have to walk by the cafeteria. That way everyone sitting there eating their no-salt, no-taste food gets a reality check.

Once I opened the door of a nursing home to go outside and leave one time. It was a solid door, and I pushed it hard to swing it open to roll the cot through the doorway. Right outside, in front of the door, unbeknownst to me, was a little old lady smoking a cigarette. She must have been standing inches in front of the door, maybe even leaning against it, because when I opened that door I sent her flying. She landed with a thud, cigarette still in her hand, and started moaning and crying. It looked like I had really hurt this little old lady.

I felt really bad, re-opened the door and yelled for help. Several nurses arrived, picked her up and took her back to her room. They told me not to worry. I said I was sorry a hundred times and left my name and the name of the funeral home where I worked. What else could I do?

Who knows, maybe she might need a funeral home?

I have heard some awful swearing coming from little old ladies in nursing homes. Naughty, naughty.

Unfortunately we live in a society that needs nursing homes, yelling take me, take me in a loud clear voice. I can't deny that. My hat goes off to the folks out there who take care of their own folks. I have met you. You are special.

Take Me

I had a little lady grab my arm while I walked down the hall of a nursing home. She grabbed hold of my arm and stopped me, and the cot I was walking with, cold. Then she started yelling "TAKE ME. TAKE ME" in a loud clear voice. I couldn't get rid of her. She wouldn't let go of my arm for nothing. This went on for a couple of minutes as I stood there. All the other patients came out of their rooms to see what the commotion was all about. The nursing staff had to come to my rescue and pry her arm from mine.

I showed up at a nursing home one time at about 4am. When I was about a block away I passed a confused-looking old man walking away from the nursing home in a hospital gown. When I arrived and walked into the nursing home, it was in a panic. It seemed one of their patients had walked off.

"NO problem!" I said. "I saw him walking down the street." I jumped back in the van with a nurse and we went and picked him up. We drove back to where he was and the nurse gently guided him back into the car. That was the only time I went to a nursing home and picked up a body that rode in the front seat of the car.

Another time I was driving back from some hospital about an hour north of town. The body in the back and I were listening to the stereo and we were getting ready to merge onto the freeway and head for home. Well, standing next to the freeway on-ramp at 3:30 in the morning was this old man, hitchhiking.

I picked him up. He had a bag with him and he said he was heading for the Y.M.C.A. He told me he was running away from a nursing home his daughter had forced him to move into.

"God Damn place," he said. "They are always sticking me with needles, and probing my ass. The food stinks, and the nurses hit me."

We talked all the way to town. He had all his faculties about him, and in my non-medical opinion, he seemed to be a normal old man.

I gladly took him to the front door of the Y.M.C.A. It was not very far out of my way.

I never told him what I did for a living, and he never looked in the back of the van. He thanked me for the ride. I often wondered how far he got.

To the good nursing homes, I tip my hat. I wish there was more of you. To the bad nursing homes out there, I hope you get sued by someone's family, fined by the government, and forced to improve the condition of your establishment. Please bring it up to the level where you are providing quality care for your patients. The kind of care you would expect for your own mother. If you can't or won't do that, close down and move away. We don't need any more piss palaces in town. One more thing: pay your help more.

Thankfully, most facilities are wonderful caring places.

Some folks just can't take care of their family like it was done in the old days. In the old days the entire family stayed together and took care of each other right up until the end.

That was then and this is now. See how times change?

The most important thing, whether you take care of your parents yourself or have a licensed facility do it for you, is to treat the elderly with respect and dignity. This is very important. They may be old and gray, but they still have something to say.

Here's another bit of advice. An old undertaker told me once that the hearing is the last to go when someone is going. So don't you go saying something stupid around your dear old mom or dad, like die, you fucking bastard! Unless you want them to hear it.

Take That

A nice-looking, relatively young lady came in one time to make arrangements for her mother. We completed the arrangements and after a while we got to talking about her father. He had died 2 years ago. Before he died, he had written a will and had listed her (his daughter) as the executrix of the will, not his wife, which would have been usual. She was one girl in a family of four kids, two girls and two boys. As the will was read, it went something like this: "… To my eldest son, who lived only 20 minutes from his parents, yet who would never bring his children to see us on Christmas, Halloween, Easter or to celebrate a birthday or even for a

Saturday afternoon, and who would never call or write I leave 50 cents. To my second son, who lived around the corner, I leave half as much…"

How about them apples? Just goes to show, you get what you deserve.

This was a wealthy man too. It made me think I had better call my parents.

Excuse Me

I had man get up during the funeral and yell, "He was a no good bastard!"

What do ya do with that?

Well, you sit back and watch what happens. That is what I did. This man was drunk, and was not-so-gently removed from the funeral home by the sons of the deceased. I didn't have to do anything. Afterwards we all got a good laugh out of it.

People show up at funerals drunk all the time. Usually, everything is cool and there is no problem. That is unless they start burping or farting. I've seen both happen a time to two. It isn't very funny. Well, it's not supposed to be funny, but when you are the undertaker standing in the back of the crowd, watching over things and you hear a big fart during a prayer, well, you have to bite your lip not to smile.

One funeral home I worked at had its only restroom available for the public situated in the family room. This was great for the family. Unfortunately everybody who also needed to take a crap or a piss had to use it too. It was a sharing moment. The door to the restroom must have been made from the lightest and thinnest of wood known to mankind: paper.

Before, during and after each funeral, each family who sat in this family room was entertained; not only by the comforting words from the preacher and the soft music from the choir, but also by the cascading fall of water, whether from high or low, the plop, plop sound of objects hitting water, next, the soft or loud sound of farts bouncing around, the gentle whoosh of the toilet paper roll, followed by a loud and powerful flush, the washing of hands, and all the rest. Every fucking time someone had to use the crapper that was our only crapper. I directed some old drunk to the restroom while a funeral was going on. He took a big loud shit and when he left, he left the door open. A family member got up and quickly closed it, but it was too late. If I could smell his shit from the back of the chapel everyone in the chapel smelled it. All the locals knew to shit and piss before coming to this funeral home for a funeral.

I went to work one day with the hangover from hell. I felt like and looked like shit. Right after I got to work a family came in to make the funeral arrangements for their mother. As the conference progressed I felt worse and worse and started to get the sweats. During the middle of writing the obituary I had to excuse myself. I ran to the sink in the preparation room and threw up. Boy, I needed that.

Like Footprints in the Sand

Have you ever had the cops stand next to you at a funeral?

I thought not.

A couple of times I have had a family request it. The family would ask me if I could please have a couple of armed police attend the funeral. This was for the protection of someone who definitely wasn't liked by someone else in the family. I have been told that there will be a shooting if so and so shows up and sees so and so. Well, I do what I am told, and so I call the cops. They come and stand ready and look good. So far, knock on wood; I have never had someone die at a funeral. But, I bet some other undertakers have a good story to tell.

The closest I came to having someone die at a funeral was a lady who popped a vein in her leg during one. We helped her out of her pew, with her leg bleeding fast, down the aisle and onto a couch in the foyer. We tied a tourniquet around her leg and helped her down another hall and into the ladies restroom. Someone called for an ambulance. While some family members helped her in the restroom the memorial service continued. The ambulance arrived with its sirens blaring and they hauled her away. The minister never missed a beat. The memorial service soon ended and everyone left with a great dead body story. We ended up with a trail of blood in the carpet from the pew to the can. It was our footprints in the sand, and you could see it for months.

Loch Ness

I rode my motorcycle to Dufftown Scotland, to visit the Glenfiddich Whiskey Distillery and sample their wares. I had earlier that day ridden around Loch Ness Lake, and was depressed because I hadn't seen Nessie, but more to this story I was really depressed because, arriving at quitting time, the distillery had closed for the day, and I missed my chance for a tour. It wasn't a total loss because the town had several pubs and friendly people. I woke up the next day after a heavy night of sampling whiskeys and found myself self quite well-preserved.

When I die, and when I'm gone, I want to be embalmed with scotch. I don't really want to be embalmed, but just in case I have to be, take a good pull from the bottle and fill me with scotch, boys. You know who I'm talking to. Yes sir, to hell with that sterile, chemical, preservative, death juice. I want something that made me live. Who knows, it might just kick start the heart. It's funny no one yet has ever requested that.

On a Hill Far Away

We used to have several retired ministers help us by conducting funerals for those folks without any preacher to call their own. These fellows were really great to work with. There are a lot of people without their own preachers.

One old minister had memorized about three funeral services. All he would do is add the name of the dead person, in all the important places, and carry on as if this person was his long lost best friend.

He did a wonderful job. Sometimes, however, he would mix up the services in his head and they would come out wrong. He would be going along, speaking very eloquently, saying; something like, "And Joe, well, Joe, would be standing there, representing a lone tree, standing tall, on a hill in a field" and, then, he would continue, "and the plane would leave the runway, and disappear into the sky, and yet somewhere on a distant shore I know a ship appears, bringing Old Joe home." It's hard to describe, but it was like he had missed a page in his sermon.

When he did that in the chapel, everybody would wake up, though. I would watch and most folks would be listening sleepily following along until they heard the mistake; Eh, what's that? Um. Excuse me? What's he talking about? Who knows, he might have been doing it on purpose.

I had a nice funeral for the wife of this very kind old man. He came in the next day or so, to settle up and pay the bill. He still looked very sad. He told me that, while he was at the funeral, some kids had broken into his home and destroyed it. They drank the booze in a cupboard, knocked over his refrigerator, knocked the cabinets off the wall in the kitchen, broke his T.V. and generally ransacked the place. I remember him saying that there were eggs leaking all over the floor, mixed in with milk. I felt very, very bad for this kind old man.

What a Goddamn shitty thing to do. You can bet it was some high school kids or junior high kids. The cops were looking into it and I hope they caught the punks.

I have breathed enough, and have spilled enough embalming fluid on me over the years, it's a wonder I'm not more fucked up. It is really scary shit. Very toxic. Very carcinogenic. I knew an old undertaker who swore that the fluid and its toxicity had made him sick. He was one of the old boys who worked his life away in a preparation room without any ventilation, using only the good shit on the dead folks.

Goldie Locks

It really shakes things up when a high school kid dies in a small town.

I conducted a funeral where the local high school star basketball player died. He thought he could drive his car around a corner marked 35 at 100mph; that didn't work. I spent several hours on that boy, to get him to look more or less like his picture.

When I was around 19, one night I was assisting with visitations. I had to greet families and show them to what we call visitation rooms, where they could take a peek at their dead person. Some undertakers call it a slumber room, but no matter. My job was to greet them, take them up the elevator to their rented room and wait guard outside in the hall until they had seen enough. Then I was to escort them back to the front door.

The body on view that night belonged to some kid who, while driving drunk, crashed very unfortunately and burned, knocking his head off in the process. The boys had him in a casket with a black plastic bag hiding his head from view. He had a suit and tie on, and other than the fact that under that black plastic bag his head looked like a cracked egg stuck on his shoulders, he looked all right. I was putting more flowers in the viewing room and had checked him out before his family came to the funeral home. Another associate of mine escorted them to his room and left me to escort them out. I waited for them to leave. They walked out, and the mother took one look at me started crying and blubbering and hanging all over me. She hugged me as hard as she was crying. She asked if I drank beer.

"No." I lied.

"You look just like our son." She said, and she started crying all over again. The father was crying, she was crying, I was the only one who wasn't crying. At that time I hadn't been to undertaker school, and was still wet behind the ears, and I didn't have anything consoling to say, so I walked them quietly to the elevator and out the door. I went back up into the viewing room. The family had brought a picture of the kid by his Chevy which they had placed on the table. By God, I did look just like him.

Same long blond curly hair. That was strange.

The old boys I worked with used to call me Goldie Locks because of my curly hair. Well, shit, it was the 70's and everybody else had a perm too.

The girls liked it.

Drinking and Not Driving

Sure, I've done it. I've also picked up lots of drunken, dead kids and adults on motorcycles, in cars, vans and buses who just weren't doing it right. One time I got a guy who T-Boned a train. The dumb fuck, his timing was a bit off, as he hit the second engine. He hit the train in a van running from the cops going over a hundred. The impact actually knocked the engine over. He was one messed up boy.

Sometimes in an accident only the passengers get killed. That makes it really shitty for the driver, who lives and sometimes isn't hurt at all.

When I was in high school a guy in an upper class died. We all went to the funeral. I really didn't even know the guy. But I knew I had to go and skip school after the funeral.

As undertakers we know that when high school kids die, you have to be ready for anything. If the family wants a visitation, all kinds of things can, and usually, do happen.

I've had, during these types of visitations, groups of kids stand outside the funeral home and drink beer. I'm sure some of them were underage and it happened more than once or twice. Most times it didn't bother me, as I am not the one to pass judgment on others. This time, however, they got the idea that they were angry at the funeral home. They started throwing their bottles at the garage wall, which caught my attention. I went outside and said "Hey, man take it easy on the place," or something like that. I wasn't going to call the cops, but I said I would if they wouldn't stop. They didn't care, it only made them madder. Their friend was dead from driving drunk into an embankment wall too fast, and that was that.

After they left I went outside and cleaned up the mess. I smiled at them at the funeral the next day. Most of them were sorry about what happened. You know what I saw after the funeral? The same bunch drinking and cruising round. Oh well, blame that one on culture. Live fast, and take lots of chances.

Still Waiting for Harry

Death is serious! When you are dead, you are DEAD. No ifs or buts about it. I have only heard of one person, maybe two, coming back from the dead; Jesus and, maybe an Apostle? I don't know. I can remember going to see the 12 Apostles off the southern coast of Australia. There are only 6 or 7 of them left.

If you come back from the dead, I mean the really, really, dig yourself out of your grave, dead, I would like to shake your hand. Call me first. I'll call up the talk shows!

First Watch

I can't say for certain what happens to your soul, but I know what happens to your ass.

My first embalming was a bloody mess. To be really honest, every embalming is a bloody mess. I had only been working in the funeral business about a week when the boss said, "Well its time you learn how to shoot the juice." We walked into the preparation room, gloved up, put gowns on and I prepared to embalm my first body, a naked old lady. He gave me a scalpel and showed me where to make a cut on her neck, "Not to big, and not to deep" he said. Well, I cut BIG and deep. Blood started running all over the place. The blood went all over her chest and down along the custom table, and into the drain. The table had grooves along the sides to allow the blood to drain, which is a good thing. If (and how often you do!) you let an arm lie in the way, as it was that day, it dams the flow of the blood, causing it to pour onto the floor. That day it really poured. We had blood everywhere, and we hadn't even started embalming. It wasn't as much blood as you may think, but it made a nice red pond on the floor. I grabbed a mop and a bucket and cleaned up the mess and in a minute the blood stopped flowing and we began again.

I'm reminded of a song: "We all need someone we can bleed on..."

I didn't think the blood would spray out all over the fucking place when I cut into this dead woman, but it does. That is because the circulatory system is under pressure and because when I stupidly cut deep, I cut the vein, thereby opening the gates and releasing the pressure. It also helped that she was freshly dead. I think she was under an hour. You are not supposed to cut deep enough to cut the artery with your first cut. The first cut is to locate them. We used a bunch of cotton and cleaned up the mess inside the hole I had made and I got to see what the inside of a neck looks like. Let me tell ya. There's a lot of red stuff in there. I stood and watched after that.

He used some other tools and started digging around inside her neck, and I used a cotton pad to soak up the blood, which was still leaking from God knows where. Pretty soon, using a hooked typed of instrument, he pulls out from inside her neck just an inch or so, a pale white, thick, cord. "The carotid artery" he said. "Jesus!" I said. I was already about sick to my stomach. He grabbed some string, and put the string around this artery, and tied a loose knot. He then went back to digging around in there and moving things this way and that, and next he pulled out a clear red transparent thin strand of something; "The jugular vein you just about cut in half" he said. He showed me where I had nicked the vein. He slid a long tool which spread apart the vein, and opened it up.

He next started to adjust her mouth; opening and closing it, and moving the lips around. He pulled out a syringe-like instrument and put in it a small sharp metal dart with a six inch wire attached. He stuck that in her mouth, up against her upper jaw, right above the teeth, and POW! The dart was stuck in her jaw! He gave the gun to me, and told me to do the same, against the lower jaw. I did, and with a touch of my trigger finger, I had stuck my first dart into the jaw of a dead person. Hundreds, if not thousands, have followed.

Using one hand to hold her mouth closed just the way he wanted, he wound the two wires together, tight. They held the mouth closed. He moved her lips into place and with her mouth closed, she looked just like she was sleeping.

We undertakers get asked all the time, how do we keep the mouths closed on people? I have heard from numerous people numerous stories. I have heard that we sew the lips together, which, we don't. I have been told we use super glue, which we do, but a special kind. The lips, I am told, are the most looked-at feature when people look at the dead. Next, are their hands? Stitching the lips would be hard to hide and probably result in a hell of a lawsuit if seen. Get the lips and hands right, and you've got it made. The last thing the undertaker wants is old granddads mouth popping open during the good bye and kissing that goes on after the funeral is over and before they close the lid.

When the jawbones are too soft to get the darts to stick, the good undertaker must use more technical procedures, which I can't speak about.

He now had the mouth looking right, and then he had me clean her fingernails. He washed her eyes, and placed upon each eye, a gray convex, ribbed plastic lens cap. It looked like a really big contact, with grooves that pricked at my fingers. "Eye Caps" he informed me. After he had placed the eye caps on, he pulled the eyelid closed over it. He smoothed the wrinkles away, and. Presto! The face of the dead looked pretty alive. When we had started, her mouth was a wide, gaping hole, and her dried-out open eyes looked dully at me. Now she looked as kind and nice as Aunt Bee. Asleep.

He filled up the tank on the embalming machine with water and into it he poured two bottles of chemicals. "Embalming Fluid, here smell this," he said, "Good for drying out coughs and colds," he said. I took a whiff. Man-o-Man! That was some bad-ass shit! Every time I had a runny nose, I took a little whiff of it and my nose would dry right up.

When he turned on the pump and I saw the amount of blood that came pouring out of this little old lady, I ran out of the room heading for the porcelain God. He never said anything 20 minutes later when I came back into the preparation room. As I stood there, I watched her blood run down the sink, and noticed that it had changed color and now it was close to the same pink juice that came from the tank, "We're just about done," he said. "Notice how the color of her skin matches the color of the fluid?" Her skin color had changed and did match the color of the embalming fluid, sort of. "That's what you want," he said. "Oh yes, very nice," he said.

Since that day, I have been like the Sun. I, too, have been giving people suntans. Their last suntan. My tans do not cause any unsightly lines, because I tan all of you and you, well, you look marvelous.

He Said "Well, let's have lunch, and then we'll come back and aspirate her." Well, I couldn't eat any lunch that day. When it comes to upholding the philosophy of eat 'til you puke, that day, I failed.

Embalming a body is one thing, but, as I was instructed in school, it is only a prerequisite to the aspiration of a body. Most of the bacteria in a body are in the stomach and guts. The guts are the guts of the matter, so to speak. These organs are supplied with blood from smaller blood vessels, and when the body is embalmed, they do not receive enough embalming fluid, to completely kill off all the bacteria that grow there.

This makes sense, because the job of most of these organs is to filter out the shit we eat before running it through our bodies, and you just can't pour oil through an oil filter fast. Hence, to properly embalm, we must also aspirate the body. And after lunch I learned how.

We undertakers, I soon found out, are a special breed. We not only have the skill, power, time, and wherewithal to change the color of your skin, we can also make you fatter or thinner. All with the turn of couple of dials, a flick of a switch, and the touch of a few buttons.

It is almost too much to have this much power.

Just kidding.

Back in the preparation room, we gloved and gowned up again and my boss pulled from a drawer a long hollow metal tube-shaped spear with a handle on one end and a very sharp point on the other. It looked to be about two and a half feet long. It also looked quite deadly to me. He attached a clear rubber hose to the end with the handle. The hose went to a faucet in the sink. He turned the water on, switched a valve, and the spear began to make sucking noises. He made a few marks on her belly, using his thumb and forefinger and her belly button as a guide, and told me to stick the 'Trocar', as it was called by professionals in the business, into her stomach, here, and push it up inside her to where her heart would be.

There, he pointed with his finger.

Well, I had never stabbed someone, anyone, live or dead. And, son of a bitch, it took me quite a while to get up the nerve to stab this lady. It seemed you could really hurt someone with this thing.

He was patiently waiting, watching me. I said a few Hail Marys and "Oh, shits," then I stabbed that Trocar in her. I pushed it in strong and deep. It came right out her back near her shoulder blade! "Easy does it!" - He said "Jesus Christ! You are not trying to kill her. Be gentle."

He then took the Trocar from me and he showed me how it was supposed to be done. Gently, he pushed it to where her heart was. That clear hose filled with dark blood and spit it out forcefully into the sink. Fuck! It was disgusting. I watched as the hose would run dark and then run clear as he moved it around inside her guts. "You must clear the lungs," he said.

Next, he pulled it almost out, turned it more vertical and stuck it back in. he was aiming for the bladder. I could tell when he hit it as the color of the tube changed to yellow and red. "We don't want her to wet her pants during the funeral" he said. Every once in a while the pointed end of the tube would plug up. You could hear the difference in the sucking sound. When this happened, he would pull the Trocar out of her stomach and pull out the bit of guts that had plugged the holes in the pointed end. These he threw into the sink and then he re-introduced the Trocar to this woman and continued aspirating. One second later her stomach deflated! Just like that. Poof! The sink ran thick with yellow goo. I bet her stomach dropped 2 inches. The old boy, after sucking out of that woman more blood than I thought a person had in them, finally turned off the machine, saying we are almost done. He was happy with the job. "Lovely. Just lovely," he said.

He then pulled off the hose attached to the Trocar and attached another one. This clear rubber hose was short, about 2 feet, and he screwed a bottle to the special end of this hose. This bottle was full of a stronger kind of embalming fluid. It's called Cavity Fluid. This fluid is used to preserve (what's left of) the organs, and the inside trunk of the body. It helps to slow down the natural order of decomposition, which helps with the preservation of the body. He pushed and pulled and wiggled that Trocar around inside her and filled her up with two bottles of that stuff. He slowly pulled out the Trocar and plugged the hole with a little white button, which was spun down into her belly with a special type of screwdriver. He washed her body and I held her as he rolled her up on her side as he washed her back and shoulders. We were finished.

A well-embalmed body may last 10 days, maybe 10 weeks, maybe 10 years. Each embalming and each body is different. If you add in the climate, the cause of death, and the overall health of the dead person, one might only last 10 hours. Lenin didn't look too bad, and he's been dead a long time.

Rotten From the Inside Out

I picked up a body one time from another funeral home that had embalmed it for us and brought it back to our funeral home. When I arrived to pick it up something was amiss. The guy said that the body was deteriorating fast. He wasn't lying either. That body was rotting from the inside out. We put it in a heavy duty body bag and away I went. You could hear it later that day popping and snapping. I asked the family during the funeral conference if this fellow had any internal digestive diseases and they said he had. That embalmed body just about doubled in size in one day, and it sounded like a pressure cooker, so as soon as we got the paperwork signed we cooked him.

A funeral home's preparation room that is not cleaned and sterilized regularly can keep an active staph virus going forever. Somehow, if you are the unlucky owner of a funeral home with that problem it will keep raising its ugly head now and again, no matter how much you clean. The virus must get into the metal or the paint, I don't know. Not all the bodies catch it either. I do know that it is almost impossible to kill and building another preparation room to eliminate the problem isn't out of the question. This body had caught that virus, we suspected, due to a rumor that that funeral home had that problem.

All Aboard That Train

I, during my travels, checked out some mosques in Fez, Casablanca, and in Marrakech, Morocco. In the middle of the medina (the market) in Fez there was one mosque where a king in his tomb lay. Only Muslims could enter there, so I didn't go inside and take a peek, for fear of being beheaded. I can say that if the king could look down from above, he would have liked the surroundings. There was a lot of gold and jewels glittering about the place.

I saw the medina in several old and interesting Moroccan cities. The snake charmers, belly dancers and the fire-eaters; I saw the whole ten yards. My first day in Casablanca I hired a taxi to take me to the coast. Along the way I asked the driver to get me some hash. He did, and for $20.00 bucks I had a thumb-sized bit of hash and I was a very happy man. Hell, the next day I rented a Mercedes with a driver to drive me around the country for two weeks. He didn't speak English and I didn't speak Arabic, but we both liked to drink and smoke hashish and we did plenty of that cruising around. He picked me up $20.00 bucks worth of hash later in the week, and it was the size of my hand. I couldn't smoke it all before I left the country, and I tried hard, so I gave the rest back to him with a nice tip.

We were stopped once for speeding. As my driver was discussing the situation with the policeman, I decided to take a picture. What a stupid thing to do. Immediately after the flash went off the cop was at the door screaming at me and reaching for the camera. I knew I had really fucked up, and I thought I was heading for a nice stay in a lovely Moroccan prison. Luckily, my driver saved my ass and through some cash and the relinquishing of the film from the camera, which he angrily stomped into the pavement, we went on our merry way again. We went right to the local bar and he and I bought 12 cans of beer. I felt out of place inside there, that's for sure. As we drove back to Casablanca, he threw our empty beer cans out the window. I can't tell you everything that I did in Morocco. It wouldn't be morally, or politically correct.

I worked in a funeral home where we used to ship out and receive several bodies a year by train. The train left at 5AM in the morning, and would arrive there at 9PM, depending on which way the dead were heading; you had to be at the train at least an hour early. Never did I see the train arrive or leave on time. Sometimes it would take three or four guys to lift a casket up and into the train car. Getting them out of the train was easier. We used gravity.

Trains are a convenient way to transport the dead within a given area, and a great way for living people to see the country. In different times of my life I've ridden trains from Spokane to Pittsburgh, from Warsaw, Poland to Moscow, Russia, from Moscow to St. Petersburg, from Warsaw to Budapest, Hungary and from Beijing, China to St. Petersburg, Russia. I don't worry about what else is on board.

The next time you are aboard a passenger jet, and you are waiting for it to leave and you are watching it get loaded with luggage, watch for a big long cardboard box, like a refrigerator box lying on its side. If you see one of these riding the rubber escalator up, into the plane and under your butt, you are sharing the friendly skies with the dead. Remember, ass, grass or cash, no one rides for free.

Up She Comes

Do you really want to dig up mom after 30 years, just to check if she still has those rosy cheeks we gave her? If so, go ahead. I have disinterred and re-buried a few caskets from the deep, dark dirt of life, and I peeked in each one to see how the old boys were doing. WOW!

There are a lot of factors that I have mentioned going on here that will determine what you get to see: the health of the person before he died, what killed him, his embalming, the environment, the casket and casket liner to name a few. I mentioned that water, specifically ground water, is the enemy, and it will turn mom into soup quicker than you think. Remember that, when you go to your local cemetery to pick out that lovely space for yourself.

Will I have to swim in my grave as well as roll over? Maybe your casket should resemble a boat. I haven't mentioned anything yet about mold spores though.

Mold Spores. What about the millions of mold spores that are floating around in the world we live in? There are plenty floating around inside the casket when the lid is closed. Mold has to eat something, reproduce, and live somewhere, doesn't it? Where do you think its new home is going to be? It ain't going to be that $5000.00 casket you bought, no sir. Believe me; mamma is going to need more makeup.

If the ground is dry, uncle Joe might come up looking a bit a like the Pharaohs of Egypt: just a bit dried out. You should check out the Valley of the Kings someday. I did. Try (not) to bribe the locals who will gladly take you down into other underground tombs, using dim flashlights with yellow lens. You'll get to see lots of dead bodies.

However, seeing old Joe swimming in his mushy casket which has just come up from 10 years in the ground is something you just have to be there to experience. Imagine the fun, hauling that dripping casket back to your funeral home, cleaning out the car, and pouring Old Joe into a new casket. Yee haw!! We cremated the old casket, in case you were wondering.

Every one of the bodies I saw looked like it had been dead since the day it went into the ground. And if they looked good dead then, great, cause they didn't look good now. As John Wayne once said, "Here's looking at ya kid."

Behind the Big Green Door

So many things go on behind that big door at the end of the hall in a funeral home that it brings out the curiosity in some folks. Everybody wants to see the embalming room, and most want to see a dead body. I've showed some to both, and both to some.

I have seen some tattoos on ladies that probably weren't meant for Joe average to see. I heard a story about a tat on a dead gal of the Pink Panther mowing her pubic hairs. You ladies out there have some fancy tattoos in places you wouldn't guess. In a song of mine a verse goes like that. The song is titled "Tombstone Todd the Undertaker". Get the CD.

Quite a while ago, I embalmed a body of an old man. Tattooed on his left forearm, done very poorly, were numbers. The numbers belonged to this man, who had seen the horrors of having lived through a concentration camp. He was Polish, and his wife verified his life's story.

How to Get Ahead

Do you know how long it takes to sew up a head?

If the phone doesn't ring, and the doorbell doesn't ding, and you find a song on the radio you can sing too, you can sew one up in about 30-45 minutes. A head that won't leak, that is. The chest takes about the same, not including tying off all the arteries and veins you have used. Nothing is worse than having the head leak blood onto the pillow of the $5000 casket you just sold. Well that's a lie. If the family sees it, then you are in deep shit and may as well hand them the keys to the place. If, fortunately, you notice the stain two seconds after you place the head on the pillow, no big problem yet. You take him back out, flip the pillow, and re-stitch the head, trying like hell not to stain the shirt collar any more, and/or ruin the $1000 suit he is wearing.

This shit happens to funeral homes so much that they sell a special cap made out of cardboard that is placed between the head and hidden beneath the pillow especially for this purpose. The best way to sew up a head is slowly, and nice and tight. And use the cap. A little music and a beer go well too.

Some funeral homes won't let you have a radio in their preparation room. I worked for one for a while. They said it was not respectful of the dead. That was ok, then, but it was the only funeral home I worked for without a radio in the preparation room.

I like a radio playing if I'm working alone on a dead body. It's still creepy to me after all these years to work alone without a radio going. I don't believe it's disrespectful at all. I ask their permission first. My guests don't mind. They have never complained. They don't even care if I'm singing off key.

Working without a radio is too silent and spooky for me. Especially at night. Who knows, maybe one will speak. Maybe, one WILL sit up and start talking "Hey, what-ya doing with that needle, bud?" The first time a dead body says something to me, it's "SEE YA! I'm out of here!" I would be the first one out the door, needle in hand.

What is Really Important?

You learn early in your undertaking career that the casket is more important than your hands. You place your hands on the corners of the casket as you move it through doorways. This is to protect the casket. You can easily place a bandage and cover the bleeding flap of skin you just tore off, but, it's very hard to cover up the very noticeable scratch you just put in the casket, usually minutes before a funeral. If you're the smart undertaker, and you are at a church, you very discreetly pull out the matching color crayon you have in your suit pocket and fix the problem. It's the same crayon that usually lies next to the others that match the caskets you sell in that all-too-important-junk-drawer. Crayons worked best for me. They came in all the right colors and they were quick and cheap. Some cosmetics work too, if you had the time. Cosmetics were much better for me for almost ruining the inside lining of caskets or the ladies dresses. It's a jolly good time around the campfire when you have to remove Aunt Bee's dress from Aunt Bee and have it dry cleaned ASAP because while you were powdering her nose you knocked the pink rose petal powder bottle over all over her dress. That pisses you off! Let me tell, ya, that pisses off the boss as well.

I worked on a nice dead lady once for quite a while. When I had her in the casket, she really looked nice. I was just finishing touching up her lipstick when I knocked over the lipstick bottle I had sat on her chest. Dark red lipstick poured down the side of her dress and onto the lining of the casket. It looked like she had been shot in the casket.

What a God Damn mess! I had to call the family, and explain what had happened and would they please bring down another dress. We would and (did) pay to have the stained one cleaned, which didn't work. We replaced the casket too.

I told the family exactly how it had happened. And I never sat another bottle or jar of cosmetics on the chest of a dressed dead person again.

Tools of the Trade

In school we were instructed that the body is not a tool chest! When you embalm a body, you use instruments and they should not be placed on the chest, it's disrespectful! It is, however a very convenient place to put them, and that's that. These are our 'Tools of the Trade.' When you need one, it's more convenient to pick it off the chest you're working on than it is to stop what you're doing, walk over to the counter, get it and walk back. They have special tables for all this stuff, if your employer has bought them. If you lay them on the table they somehow end up covered in blood and stuff. Tools left on a table will hide from you too. I have had to lift up and look under many a shoulder and ass to find an instrument which, due to my moving the body about, and the flow of water and blood running down the sides of table, had gone A.W.O.L.

I won't disgust you with the uses of all the tools of the trade, but I will let you in on one secret. I might know why some of you died. I about puke each time when I'm embalming you, and I can't. The reason? Your veins are so full of shit, the embalming fluid can't flow. I must reach into the vein with this special tool to squeeze out some of the ugliest, looking clots seen by man. It's no fucking wonder your dead. The old boys called the 'em, chicken clots, cause that's what they looked like.

I wouldn't mind you placing your tools on my chest if it keeps you from looking at my ass. Do you really think the dead person would mind, you putting tools on their chest? I've asked several dead people this question and I've had no complaints. I have found some instruments left in the bodies of people I have swept out of the crematory...

I worked with a guy who had a gold set of embalming instruments. They were set in a leather pouch. Each instrument had its own place. I don't think he ever used them. But we were ready if ever the case came and the person had requested to be embalmed only with gold instruments.

Fresh Spring Flowers

In the old days, all the boys would just leave the keys in the ignition of the funeral cars when we were conducting a funeral. That way they would always be there and you wouldn't have to look for them. That's the way I was instructed.

I was working one of my first funerals ever. I had been instructed to drive the flower car, a black Mercury station wagon, which was full of flower and flower stands, to the church. I did. I left the keys in the ignition as instructed and unloaded the car. I set up the flower stands in the front of the church and placed the flowers on them. The funeral had just started when one of the guys, who had been outside smoking a cigarette, said "Where's the station wagon?" "Well, right outside beside the church," I said. "Nope, its not there," he said. And, sure enough, it was gone. The funeral went off well; nobody knew anything about it until later on. Later that day the police found the car, wedged in between two trees in a trail in the woods. Two kids confessed to taking it from the church. They said the keys were hanging in the ignition. After that we always kept the keys on the visor.

When I began in the business, about the only thing I was smart enough to do was deal with flowers. I would identify the type of flowers that arrived at the funeral home and write their description on the back of the attached card. After that I would place them in their appropriate places, either the chapel or the viewing room. When we would have a funeral I would bring all the flowers from the viewing room and arrange them on flower stands in the chapel.

Identifying flowers is easy. Spelling the names of flowers is a bitch. I still have a hard time just pronouncing the names of some. Due to my self-imposed flower-spelling impediment, when chrysanthemums or cyclamens would arrive I would, as the old boys would, write on the cards: fresh spring flowers. When you arrange the flowers, you have to make them look nice. You can't just arrange them haphazardly. The colors have to blend, not clash. All the arrangements have to face the front, and not be backward on the stand. This is all very important to the undertaker and it makes a nice picture for the family, as they walk in the chapel.

After the funeral started, and everybody was seated in the chapel, we would leave. The old boys and I would jump in one of the limos and drive over to a cafe and have coffee and donuts. We would stay about 15 minutes, and then go back to the church. You can't do that now. Nowadays, we stay until they say the last Amen.

After the funeral was over I would load all the flowers back into a van, and rush them before everybody in the procession would arrive, out to the cemetery. The graveside would look oh so nice for the folks as they cruised up and parked.

I have raced up the road, heading for the cemetery, driving like a bat out of hell, and set the flowers up at the wrong gravesite. Twice.

The first time, I went to the cemetery, I set everything up all wonderful like, at a newly dug gravesite, and then watched as the procession slowly passed me by, and went on down the road. My boss, who was driving the hearse, looked at me, waving his arms and pointing in amazement! Wrong grave, you dumb shit! Well, I immediately loaded everything, and drove over parked behind all the cars. The family and other undertakers quickly placed the flowers around the gravesite. Everybody knew I was the fool.

The second time, I was standing at the door of a beautiful mausoleum, the flowers nicely adorning a space in a wall that was hidden by curtains. I should have been outside, at the gravesite.

When you load flower arrangements into the back of a hearse you have to be careful. You mustn't be in a hurry and just set them carelessly alongside the casket. Because, if you are in a hurry, and load them loosely, any which way, sure as God made little green apples, one will fall over. Three things usually happen next:

First: The first arrangement knocks over another, and then another.

Second: out pours gallons of water.

Third: all the flowers come out of their Styrofoam holders, float around and get smashed.

I have had a couple of caskets practically floating in a bath of rose petals. This might sound nice but it makes a real mess and it looks real good when you swing open the back door of the hearse and half the flowers and water pour out.

Here's the trick. It's another trick of the trade the old boys taught me early on. You pour the water out before you put them in the hearse, or flower car. Then you load them tight. The flowers arrive looking nice and orderly at their destination, there's no mess, and it looks good. It also looks good to do this when you load the flowers into the family's cars. The men folk like this. I kindly remind them to please add water when they get home

The Need for Pre-Arrangements

I heard a story about a man who walked into a funeral home and made a pre-arrangement for himself. He wanted a simple cremation with no services. He paid for it in cash. After it was all said and done he stood up, shook hands with the undertaker, walked outside, pulled out a gun and shot himself in the head, right there on the front steps. See what undertakers have to go through! Man, I'm glad that hasn't happened to me. Hopefully it was a small caliber pistol. Those big guns make a big mess.

The A.B.C.'s of Cuba

I went to Havana, Cuba, and spent a week sight-seeing and drinking. Drinking mostly at the Restaurant Floridita, drinking Margaritas, smoking Cuban cigars, and pretending I was Ernest Hemingway. If I got to the bar early enough I could sit on the bar stool next to Ernest's. His bar stool is sectioned off. Many other tourists also visit this bar and I'm sure I'm in many of their pictures. As Americans, we are not supposed to go to Cuba, so of course, I wanted to go. I flew over from Jamaica. The Jamaicans know all the tricks to getting Americans into Cuba.

While in Jamaica, I met a guy, who knew a guy, who rented apartments in Havana. A few phone calls were made and I got on the plane in Montego Bay, and got off in Havana. There, after landing, as we rolled along the runway, I looked out and saw the remains of a crashed airliner. My cousin had told me about that plane when he flew into Havana ten years ago. I bet it is still there.

I got off the plane and met another American. She was also there to take in the sights. We waited in line with 60 other people for customs clearance. Out of nowhere came a lovely little doggie that began smelling everybody's luggage. I knew what he was looking for, and I was happy I had left the stuff back at my digs in Negril.

On the proper visa, coming from Jamaica, I listed my occupation as a mortician. When I went through customs, they read my visa and I was taken aside. They thought mortician meant I had something to do with money. I was searched, asked many questions and delayed for half an hour. In the end, after I explained what I did, they smiled. Now they understood.

I had made arrangements with the owner of the apartment to meet him at a hotel. I grabbed a cab and rode into town. I used the phone in the hotel lobby in the center of Havana, and called my new landlord. In no time at all a small man was outside to greet me. He spoke English, and together we went into the apartment building across the street. We rode a very tired elevator, got out, and he knocked on the door of my new home. Out came a little old lady with a suitcase. "She lives here and she is going to stay at her sisters' while you are staying here," he said. I watched as the little old Cuban lady left carrying a small packed bag. He left and said he would come back in an hour and start the tour of his city.

My place wasn't too bad. Air-conditioned, a color TV, and it had a nice view from the balcony. It looked down the street to the fancy hotel used by all the famous dead celebrities.

My new landlord became my tour guide and friend. We had a great time. I watched the ceremonial cannon fired at the end of each day, marking the night time closing of the harbor. A similar cannon fired here a couple of weeks earlier had blown up and killed a bunch of tourists.

He took me to an old church. Inside, as we were walking around I came upon a glass section in the floor. Down through the glass I could see several coffins. It was the first of many times of seeing these during my travels. In the old times, people were buried under the floors and in the walls of churches. You were closer to God that way. The only problem with that was that there wasn't enough room in the church to bury all the folks. During those times, if you were important and/or had money and/or connections or all the above, you could still be buried there. When this was going on, it must have been a stinky place. Imagine: church services on Sunday, on Monday dig up the floors and bury a big shot on Tuesday. If you go into any old church in Europe, look closely. They will be there. Most of them will be the Hotel California of the rich and famous. It's true.

There is a theory (which may be miles from the truth) about the issue of smelling up the churches. What would you do if your church smelled like rotting corpses? Bodies buried everywhere, just a few feet under the floor. What would you do?

Incense. What better way is there to purify souls, and, get rid of the smell?

I saw all the sight and sounds of Havana and admired all the good old American cars still being driven around. Then I decided to check out a Cuban Funeral Home.

My guide found the address of a funeral home that was close. We walked to it. It was a big old, three-storied place. It looked very busy and not very well kept up. We walked inside. I, through my interpreter, met the manager who showed us around.

The funeral home had three chapels; A, B, and C; one for the poor, one for the middle class, (in Cuba?) and, one for dignitaries, the famous, and the rich people. To tell you the truth, each chapel was old and tacky. Their fanciest chapel wasn't very fancy. But, this is Cuba, remember. The only real difference between them was the wicker chairs in the poor chapel were made out of bamboo, and were all broken and scratched. The middle class chapel had few of these wicker chairs, along with some torn leather couches, scratched wooden chairs, and some curtains on the walls. The four-star deluxe chapel on the third floor had nice leather couches, lightly nicked hardwood chairs, a nice floor. There was no public elevator in the place.

It was very interesting to hear how the dead are dealt with in Cuba. Because I didn't speak the language, I listened as the funeral director told my friend, who translated everything to me.

The funeral home handled around 500 bodies a year with a staff of 18. Most bodies are not embalmed and are buried within 3 days.

It was a very cut and dry funeral home. They didn't have a casket selection room. The casket came in only one color, black. No choices. Old Henry Ford would be proud. The government pays for most of the funerals, unless you're a foreigner or have money. Burning dead people wasn't popular yet, and there was only one crematory in Havana. For those folks, choices were limited.

We stayed about an hour, and I watched one funeral leave for a cemetery. The staff was very kind and excited. I was the first American to ever stop by. Unfortunately, the manager was busy so I didn't get to see any of the, in your face, behind the door, dead of Cuba.

In America you can pick and choose, from hundreds of choices, down to the smallest detail, everything concerning your own funeral. In Cuba the choices are made for you. Which was is better?

Money Talks, Bullshit Walks

Funeral homes can be reasonable or ridiculous in their pricing. Remember, in the land of profit, profit is the King. It is good to be King. There IS profit in funeral homes.

A $4000 casket costs around a grand, maybe a bit more. The mark up in the business is usually three to four times. You pay $2500 bucks for the professional services charge and you are covering the overhead, which includes all the bills, their salary and mine (thank you very much!). Most funeral home owners are making money. Don't let anybody kid you about that. How they spend it, or save it, is up to them. It is a good living, even for the lonely peons, like me.

This is America. It costs a lot to live and die here.

There was a book written back in the eighties about the high cost of dying. It opened the eyes of John Q. Public. It also opened the eyes of Mr. Funeral Home Owner. His industry was made to look bad. We are not bad. You need our services - we want your money. Things haven't changed. If you want a bargain, you just need to look before you die. There are bargains out there. Most of the funeral homes have had to change just to survive the changing economic times. That book, which benefitted society, really pissed off the funeral industry.

Price Wars

One day, direct cremation was $1250. Within six months that went down, in stages, to $695. Two years later, it was back up to $1400. This is what might be called funeral price wars. In the western world they call it the price of having competition. A few funeral homes advertise their prices publicly, using TV, radio, and newspapers. When their prices go down, so do ours; their prices go back up, so do ours.

I remember many times coming to work and being shown a new price list, which was to start today. Now, if you were lucky and died yesterday, you saved your family lots of money. If you died today, well, expect to pay almost twice as much. Now, if you died last year, you'd have really saved your family some money, then.

The only thing worse than working for a business making a profit is not being included in its profits. When the help works 70-hour weeks for weeks on end for a 40 hour weekly salary, somebody's being exploited. That might also explain the two-day beard your local undertaker staff person is sporting. So the next time you deal with the staff please remember, they are just working stiffs, just like you.

I know a story where the owners of the funeral home would take off for months on end and leave the staff to handle things. They would tell the help the day they left, saying something like; "Say, there Joe, me and the Misses are leaving for Arizona for the winter so, hold down the fort, will ya?" And away they would go. As the years passed, and the owners vacationed, this fellow ended up assisting all the families in the community and took on the role of the undertaker in town. When the vacations finally hit the fan, he left. Soon afterwards this town, which had for 60 years only one mom and pop funeral home, had two. Within a few years, that fellow had taken away 85% of the business from the first funeral home.

Here is some good news. When you're dead - no worries.

The only difference between the rich and me is money.

I saw a sign once. It showed a picture of a bum lying in the gutter with an empty bottle of wine by his side. The caption read:

> When I was in business, I always sold cheapest.

People are going to eat, get sick and die. If you get into any of these preceding occupations you are almost guaranteed job security. You need funeral homes and funeral homes need you. It's as simple as that.

You can go cheap, skip the undertaker and lie down in a ditch and die. But please, take a moment, and think about the poor old undertaker who gets to lift your soggy sack of shit up and out of a ditch.

Who Gets the Money?

A lawsuit, for a funeral home, is very bad publicity. You could call it a no-win situation, even if the funeral home is in the right. When someone doesn't pay us, we can't repossess. If we take someone to court for not paying the bill, you can bet your last dollar, that person will be badmouthing us 'til the day they die. There is a hidden blessing in this however.

The hidden blessing is when he dies. When that happens, we won't have to bury his ass. Hell no, he'll go across the street and stiff our competition. We talk to our competition about the people who don't pay us. We know who you are.

I have had people look me straight in the eye, right after the nicest funeral you could imagine, and say they will be in tomorrow to pay in full. I never see them in the place again. Sometimes they live in the same town. I say hello to them at the grocery store. Some are embarrassed and start mumbling excuses to me in the checkout line. Others pretend it doesn't exist. When that happens, I make small talk and go back to my office and send them another bill. Funeral homes are now asking for payment upfront and in full, but that usually is a lot of cash for folks to have. Some folks tell you they can't pay you until they get the life insurance money, or their inheritance. So you say: "All right, that will be just fine. Thank you very much."

When you get good at judging people you can tell right off who will pay and who won't. It's really surprising. The little old lady who wears old clothes and drives an old car will pay you in cold cash. The shiny-shoed suit types are usually the deadbeats.

An old lady in the business once told me: "If you don't get the money in two months, you'll never see it." This makes sense. Dad is now dead and buried, and the insurance money that showed up a month ago is long gone. Who cares about the funeral home?

I knew a rich kid undertaker. His daddy owned a lot of funeral homes. For a while he had personalized license plates on his car that said Cold Cash. It looked nice on his new Beamer. At least for a while it did, until his father saw it. Then they were gone. In a big city that would have gone over fine and dandy, but this was a semi-small town. People noticed it. I noticed it parked in the funeral home parking lot.

Another kid I knew had a rich daddy who bought him a nice pop stand. He put the whole outfit up his nose.

I wanted to have "TROCAR" put on my license plates. But I haven't had the guts. I wonder how many heads that would turn?

I knew another undertaker who would buy a new Caddy every three years. He would store the new caddy in his garage for one whole year and not drive it. He would drive the old one. A year later he would sell the old one and drive the two year old one. He didn't want to appear pretentious driving a new caddy in his small community.

An undertaker driving a new Caddy? Now there's showing your families where their money goes.

Right Outta the Box

I started my working life at fifteen, as a box boy in a local grocery store. At sixteen, I moved up and started working in a gas station. One day a man drives up in a Cadillac hearse. He was a cowboy, a rodeo junkie. The hearse, he said, was his home on the road. Inside it were saddles, tack, sleeping bags, a mattress, a couple of coolers, a bean bag chair and various other odds and ends. He said it was great on the road, very comfortable, and big enough to have a party in.

It was also while I was working at the gas station that my father and some partners purchased a funeral home. It was 300 miles away from home. As a kid, I liked to drive there. Two years later, I was working in a funeral home.

Hot-Rodding the Hearse

I like old cars. Cars from the 40's 50's and 60's, even funeral cars from that era turn my crank. I would love to have a 40's hearse or a 1937 Packard Limo.

We had an early '64 black Caddy hearse at one funeral home I worked for. That baby could and would squeal the tires anytime you wanted. We had the matching limo and that baby could fly as well. Much to the shock and amazement of the lay people stopped at traffic lights looking at me, I used to squeal the tires on the coach and limo when the light turned green and speed away. Another fun thing to do when the old folks were staring you down was to pretend you were having a heart attack. The key thing to remember is to remove the name plate from the side windows of the hearse. Unfortunately, one of the owners totaled the limo and later we sold and replaced the hearse. The new owner loved that old hearse. I met up with it once on the freeway, years later, and I pulled up alongside. It was shiny black and still looking good. I gave him the thumbs up. He waved back.

Trick or Treat

One Halloween night I went to the funeral home, got the hearse, and parked it out in front of my local bar. My buddies wanted me to bring a casket into the place to add to the ambience, and set it up on the pool table. The bar owner didn't think it was a good idea.

When the seventies gas crisis came, the funeral automotive industry produced smaller hearses and limos. They did the job, but the hearses had roofs that were lower than before. They wouldn't accommodate you if you were loading a casket into them with the fancy flowery casket piece on. If you didn't remove it after the funeral, and the pallbearers were in a hurry, the casket piece would get crushed against the roofline of the car as they pushed the casket into the back. I've had that happen. One time the casket piece, after hitting the car, slid off and stained a pallbearer's suit.

A good hearse driver should be able to drive from the funeral to the cemetery with the casket piece staying on the casket. Many casket pieces don't make it that far, and end up in a heap alongside the casket. You have to be a very smooth driver. Remember, the family is following, right on your bumper. They watch your every movement.

We had a guy one time drive the hearse to the cemetery. He was filling in as an extra driver. The boss said "Just follow me in the pallbearer's car." He did a fine job of driving. He also put on a fine show the procession got to see. As we rolled merrily along, his right hand was on the wheel but his left hand was waving up and down outside the window playing with the wind. He kept his left hand out the window the whole trip playing with the wind until we pulled into the cemetery. The entire procession saw that. It looked real professional.

An old co-worker of mine chewed tobacco. When he and I were in the hearse, most of the time no one noticed his spitting the juice out the hearse window. If he was driving, he would wait until we turned away from the family and spit. Sometimes they did notice and sometimes you could see the juice stain on the door.

Stop That Cough'n

More than once I have forgotten to put in the pin which holds the casket in place inside the hearse. Without it, the casket will, as you stop and go, roll backwards: Bang! And forwards: Bang! Depending on how you drive, this could be disastrous. I have driven to a few cemeteries with one hand one the wheel and the other holding onto the casket to keep it from slamming into the back door, popping it open, and falling out on the street. I've heard of this happening to other unfortunate undertakers. Having this happen would be one of the top ten things not to do.

Driving to the cemetery is standard operating procedure for the undertaker. Driving to the right cemetery is a different story.

I was in the lead car, the Pallbearers car, and we were heading for a cemetery. I had about 20 cars following behind me in the procession. We had police escorts on motorcycles stopping traffic for us and they delivered us to the spot. However, there were two cemeteries, each sitting right across the street from each other.

You guessed it ... I drove into the wrong one leading the cars. This really screwed things up for a while until all the cars could get turned around.

This happened at my grandfather's funeral. As the procession was cruising down the freeway, heading for the cemetery, my cousin driving his car behind the family limo decided to take an early exit. All the cars followed him, right into the drive-through of Burger King. He was hungry and thought he could pick up a quick couple of whoppers before going to the cemetery. I bet my grandfather laughed over that one.

Have you ever noticed that only very old men get to be pallbearers? Granted, they were probably the close friends of the deceased. I have, over the years, watched several elderly pallbearers over-extend themselves lifting and carrying their friend. Two old boys limped back to their cars in severe pain. It's a wonder some of them don't have a heart attack doing this.

I had one close call, but I've never had the pallbearers completely drop the casket.

One time, I had a graveside service on a terribly windy, bitter cold day. A foot of snow had fallen by early morning and was still coming down hard. The service was at 11AM. The cemetery was on a hill way out in the country. The coach (what we professionals prefer to call the hearse) wouldn't have made it up the hill to the gravesite. The road had been plowed but had drifted in again. We had to carry the casket. The youngest pallbearer was about 70. I asked if they all thought they were up to the task, and they all said yes. It was a long way up the road and then a short, steep climb down the other side to the grave. Total distance: 250, maybe 300 yards. Off into the blizzard went the party of 20 or so family members and us.

You can always pick out the undertakers at a cemetery. We're the ones with the thick winter coats, the hats, the gloves, and the rubber galoshes. This ain't our first rodeo. We come prepared for the weather. These old boys were not.

Well, a few of these boys were wearing boots. Nobody had gloves. By the time we slugged our way halfway up the hill through the deep snow everybody, including me, was pooped out. I was dripping with sweat.

A good undertaker always takes hold of the proper end of the casket in these kinds of situations and for once I disobeyed that rule and I was on the head end, in front, blazing the trail, walking semi-backwards making a trail in the snow. I was trying to lift as much weight to help these boys as possible. I didn't want to kill them. We set the casket down in the snow so they could rest, near the top of the hill. After about 5 minutes or so, off we went again. At the top of the hill, we rested again. Now came the fun part.

The gravesite was on the north side of a steep hill overlooking the valley. A wonderful spot indeed. Very panoramic. Today, it was covered with ice and the wind had made a long low snowdrift around the headstone. The walkway shoveled out by the cemetery guys was only a faint trace in the snow. I changed sides and grabbed the uphill side of the casket. I planned to be the brake if needed. When everybody was ready, down we slid. Slowly, step by step, we went down the hill. How we got the casket to the grave without dropping it, I don't know, but we did. One guy would slip and fall, and we would grunt and hold on until he got up and grabbed hold of his bar. Then another would slip. It was tough going. When we neared the gravesite, we stopped and rested again. They were all very cold and tired but they wouldn't change places when asked by the younger men in attendance. We couldn't lift the casket over the drift so we slid old Joe's casket over the snow and then placed it neatly on the lowering device and began the service. There was a large gap between the hole in the ground and the lowering device that day. Those boys don't know just how close they came to having one foot in the grave.

I've always feared one day that would happen to me. The sun would be shining. The family would be following and everything would be going along perfectly until, the boys placed the casket on the grave. Then the ground around the grave would give away and one would slip and fall in. This has happened to many undertakers, I've been told. I also heard about the straps breaking, dropping the casket from its resting place on the lowering device. I would love to see it happen and not be the man in charge.

Old Glory

When you watch military funerals on TV, notice them folding the flag they give to the family. It comes out perfect every time. A perfectly folded American flag is all blue. No red or white stripes.
There is a special team of military personnel that perform this duty for the dead armed servicemen and women. Their job is to be professional. They also have a complete unit of men. They fold it, and press it, and fold it, and out comes a perfect blue triangle.

When it's done locally it is usually done by The Veterans of Foreign Wars or The American Legion, or by us jokers.

I take my hat off to the boys in these organizations. They will come to any cemetery with just a few days notice. There, they will stand at attention until their job is completed in weather you wouldn't want your dog to be out in. They fold the flag, present it to the family, fire a 21-gun salute and play taps. All to honor all fallen veterans, anywhere, anytime. Bravo! I commend them for their diligence.

However, these organizations aren't filling up as fast anymore with young veterans. Traditionally, WWII boys would arrive at the cemetery. The best of the best, they were, the youngest being a sprite 70 or so. It's tough on some of them just to show up. They usually don't have ten extra hands to help fold the flag. They fold the flag with two men. It's hard for some of them just to walk from the bus to the gravesite and back. They fold the flag with the same if not more solemn respect than the boys on TV show, and that's that. It is funny, though, that almost without a doubt, when they perform the 21-gun salute not all of the rifles will fire. Many times one or two rifles will misfire. A 21-gun salute becomes a 17 or

18 gun salute. The honor guard is always an honor to watch.

I have folded the flag backwards, meaning, starting at the stars, and I have started folding it left to right instead of right to left. This was done each time in front of a crowd of people, and each time I had to unfold it and start over. That's one way to make you look stupid. There is a technique to it. If you follow it, the flag will almost always come out perfect.

Once I saw the flag slip from the men's fingers and fly away. Then they played taps.

I have heard taps played so well at the cemetery it moved me. I have also heard it played so bad it was embarrassing.

Dead Famous People

I visited the city cemetery in Vienna, Austria. I wanted to have my picture taken playing my guitar at Beethoven's grave. It was a beautiful day. The taxi driver drove me right to the spot. Many people visit here. Flowers surrounded an iron fence. There is a big marble headstone, with his picture on it. He is buried next to Mozart, Schubert and other famous musicians. I stood there, and to be different, played Bouree in E minor, by Johann Sebastian Bach. I wondered if old Ludwig rolled over in his grave. There were some old ladies sitting on a park bench close by listening and watching my antics. They looked chagrined. So, as to not spoil my Karma, I played for all to hear, Fur Elise, by Beethoven.

They really like to use granite and marble in Europe. Every cemetery I visited had hundreds of huge markers carved from marble or granite. In America for the average Joe, these headstones would cost half a year's salary. Almost every grave in the cemetery in Vienna had a headstone that was six to eight feet tall. They were very fancy, with sculptures of angels, and animals. When you are in Europe you know you're getting close to a cemetery, because as you get nearer you start to see headstone stores, and flower shops, all displaying and selling their wares.

Life in Luxor, Egypt

Get yourself to Luxor, Egypt. When you check out the Luxor Temple, do go at night. It's a wonderful sight to see. The Luxor Temple was found hiding in the sands below the ruins of another temple. As you walk through the centuries-old columns and look toward the Nile you'll get to see a big neon McDonald's sign. I imagined as I closed my eyes the old fry cooks slaving over the ovens frying up cheeseburgers, McNuggets and fries for their kings. What a party that must have been! Young King Tut had it made! I didn't know he was the founder of McDonald's, or that it was that old, but there it was; right next to a 6,000-year-old temple. I wanted a picture but I had run out of film.

The Life of Flowers

One time I just about swallowed a pin. It was holding the card to the flower arrangement, and I was removing the card. I was in the front of the chapel after the service had ended and we were loading up to go to the cemetery. There were only a few people in the chapel milling about when I put the pin into my mouth to hold on to it while I wrote the description of the flowers onto the back of the card. The flowers had arrived without said description, a job that BELONGS to the florist. We were just about loaded up and ready to leave. Well, for some reason or another I just about swallowed that pin. It was stuck way back in my throat. I started gagging and luckily it popped out. That looked real good. It's a bitch having to write eloquently and quickly spell correctly the descriptions of flowers. Like I have said, I don't know all the kinds of flowers there are, so I write anything close.

Usually there are two kinds of undertakers when it comes to flower arranging. The first wants the flower cards removed before the service starts, so that the flower arrangements look better. The second wants them left on. I prefer to leave them on. It doesn't matter. Just as soon as you remove the flower cards to give them to the family, someone will come up and ask to see who sent what. Some people will tell me, "I ordered some roses and these can't possibly be the ones I ordered. They look terrible. May I see the card, please?" So I have to go and look through the envelopes and match up the one she is asking about.

I have noticed people changing the cards from a small plant they must have sent, to a big plant.

I didn't say anything.

Did you know that there are grades of flowers and funeral flowers are at the bottom? When you order flowers for a funeral you get the bottom of the barrel. Sometimes they are so dead, they look worse than the dead guy. Even I have noticed and have had to call the flower shop to complain.

When I first started in this business, I couldn't imagine the cost of flowers. Flowers are expensive! We used to have a flower shop in a funeral home I worked for. After funerals I was often told to throw away all the flowers. Fresh roses, lilies and all kind of flowers that really looked nice. I used to take the roses and give them to my girlfriends. I kept some nice plants too. I would take to the garbage dozens of roses, carnations, plants, and arrangements. What a waste! Hell, that didn't make any sense to an 18-year-old kid looking to get laid. And what better way to get laid, than to give the girl roses. My girlfriends loved me. This went on for quite a while until we got caught. That was the end of that. Nowadays, we ask the family where we can deliver the flowers. Usually they go to nursing homes and hospitals. I have dropped off hundreds of flowers at nursing homes and know that the residents there know these are funeral flowers.

All in the Family

The day my grandparents held their 60th wedding anniversary party my grandpa had cut his thumb. He had a bandage on it and he and I were getting all gussied up for the party. He couldn't get his tie to tie right. He asked me for some help, and I told him to lie down. He laughed at that for a long time and told it to all his friends. My grandfather was 84 when he died. He weighed over 360 pounds. He was very proud of the fact that he had been married 63 years and had owned 61 new cars.

Bloody England

I went to a funeral home in England once. Over there they still do things the old-fashioned way. The caskets arrive as finished wood boxes. No fancy silk-lined, down-filled, satin-covered interiors with the oversized pillows from the factory installed and ready to lie down in. This is how we get them in the good old U.S.A. No sir, in merry old England when I was there they had to install the interiors and attach all the handles and rails to the outside of each casket. I talked to one undertaker. "We have to be carpenters, and interior decorators," he told me. "Half the time the handles won't fit the casket or the lining is not cut right, and we have to alter it. You Americans have it made."

Their caskets were shaped like the coffins you see in good old horror flicks. In America, our caskets have the design pattern of a shiny refrigerator. Theirs had style, in that old-fashioned, Dracula kind of way. The only thing that bothered me was they didn't seem very big. England is a fat country. I wonder how someone my grandfather's size would have fit and looked comfortable. Even someone my size would be a tight fit.

Here's Looking at You, Kid

Looking right in a casket is very important. I bet most people don't think a bit about it, but we, the promoters of seeing the dead, do.

If you don't have the head adjusted right, it won't look natural. If the chin is touching the neck, that won't look normal. If the head is tilted back so far you could look up their nostrils, that ain't right either. There is a trick to adjusting the head; you must make sure the nose is level.

The next time you attend a buddy's funeral bring a small level and check.

How about those hands? Where the hell should they go? Some undertakers lay them down the side along the body. Others fold them over the waist. I have seen the right one over the heart and the left one down the side. Some place flowers in the hands, others, a book. Left hand over right or right hand over left? Was the dead person married? If so, do you want the wedding band to show?

Hands are very tricky to place right. Sometimes the fingers are bent unnaturally. Other times the fingers are spread too far apart from each other. That looks unnatural too. Who cleans under the nails, so the person doesn't look like they've been digging their own grave? Who picks out the fingernail polish if one hasn't been provided? We do all that.

I have put a beer in the hands of some, a cigarette in the hands of others.

I had a guy call up and say his friend was about to die and could we customize a casket for his friend. "Sure" I said. "What would you like?" He wanted a stereo with speakers installed and the Rolls Royce Grill from his soon-to-be-dead buddy's Rolls, mounted on the foot end of the casket. He also wanted to have his friend buried with his guitar and amp. I said we could do all that. We never heard back from that guy and I wonder if his friend died and got his wish.

Nowadays undertakers realize that accommodating people's unusual requests is just a part of the business. I have always believed in it, and I have gotten into trouble for doing so.

I had a family one time want to toast their dead friend at the end of the service. 'Sure', I said. No problem. Well, the problem was the toast turned into a drunk, because they and I toasted this guy for hours.

After several drinks, I was as toasted as the rest. Everybody was laughing and singing and having a great old time. Then my boss walked in. He wanted to check out why the lights were still on hours after the funeral. I thought I was in deep shit for fraternizing with the family. We, dignified undertakers, did not do such things with families. And besides, drinking in the funeral home is disrespectful of the dead and probably illegal. And I was supposed to be working, for God's sake. My boss wasn't really that mad; he had a drink with the family, and left me to clean up the place.

Those Guys in That Profession

There are undertakers who drink and a few who don't. There are undertakers who look like Herman Munster, Digger O'Dell and Percy Crump. And still others who resemble Joe Average. Some are normal undertakers, and some are strange motherfuckers.

When I went to Mortuary College, I was probably one of the strangest of all. All I owned was my Harley. I would walk into class every day in leathers and boots. If it was raining, I would leave a puddle. Most of the other guys in class would wear suits.

We would have to attend funeral conventions, go to casket factories and funeral homes. There we would meet the people in the industry who made everything tick. A day before we left for our first conference, one guy spoke up, and asked, "Should we wear suits?" "Yes" said the instructor. I think the kid was looking at me. I rode to the designated place in the rain the next day, and in my soaking wet leathers, walked inside and dripped water all over the carpet of the funeral home. Everybody from the owner of the funeral home, to the instructor, to my fellow classmates looked at me like I was a low-down piece of shit. Nobody would stand by or talk to me. When the owner of the funeral home was done telling us about the wonders of being a funeral director he asked for questions. I was the only one who spoke. I asked him how much he pays his help. Let me tell you, that went over like a nun in a whorehouse. I wanted to know but I never did find out.

Some of my classmates also wore hats to school and smoked fancy pipes. They looked like copies of Sherlock

Holmes. They looked real cool marching two by two into and out of the school cafeteria. Some of these boys had never seen a dead body before.

I learned in mortuary school that girls like guys with Harleys. I love girls who like guys with Harleys. And I did.

For the class picture, we were all supposed to wear our finest duds. I wore jeans and a tee shirt. The photographer luckily positioned me so that I am not seen in the picture.

On the last day of school, after I had finished my finals and was standing outside the classroom, a classmate came out and asked if I would like to go have a beer? "Sure, Hell Yes!" I said. We had never said more than two words to each other during the past year. We have been friends ever since.

He worked for a while at a very old funeral home in the same city as I, and we partied there often in its cool old mausoleum, buried down in the basement. The underground mausoleum had a deep sink that was used to fill up flower baskets with water. There were still very old urns behind glass and brass watching over us in this creepy old place. The water had long ago been turned off. He went over to the sink and unscrewed the J-shaped water flute and turned it over. He filled the short end with some pot, added some water in the other end and Presto! We had a bong! Now you know why we partied down there.

Showtime

Once the funeral starts, we get to stand back and watch what happens. Usually, someone shows up late. Half the time it's a son or daughter.

At some funerals, some folks get up and get into it. They dance around and sing. I watched a big old gal once, stand up, yell, scream and then fall to the ground. She kept on chanting on and on, while she was lying in the aisle of the church. Her family picked her up and sat her down in the pew. A couple of minutes later, she jumped up, and started yelling, and chanting, and then she fell down again.

She was either overcome with emotion, or she was the leader of the pack. After her second performance, it caught on. Other ladies started doing the same thing. The men were running from lady to lady trying to keep them standing and the women kept falling down. The preacher was preaching and the people were screaming. It was quite a circus. Old ladies were rolling around the floor and the choir was singing. It was a hell of a funeral. My partner and I watched with stone faces and laughing hearts.

An old boy told me of a funeral he had conducted a long time ago. It was a Catholic funeral. During the service, everybody is fed the flesh of Christ in the shape of a wafer and then given, to wash this down, the blood of Christ represented by red wine. At the conclusion of this in-service snack, the priest feeds himself and also takes a drink. This time, the wine accidentally went down the wrong pipe. Up violently it came, all over the pall covering the casket, and all over the family sitting in the front row, a fountain of wine. My friend said he just about fell over laughing. That was, of course, after he left the chapel, and went somewhere out of sight and sound.

Living Amongst the Dead

Almost all the old funeral homes were built with apartments where either the owners or staff lived and waited for the phone to ring. I have lived in several funeral homes. I have lived in nice ones and not-so-nice ones. In the early days when phones were still a novelty someone had to be by that phone, 24 hours a day, and seven days a week. They didn't have call-forwarding, pagers, cellphones or computers. All these new-fangled items make the life of an undertaker much easier.

Initially the owners probably lived in these apartments. That is, until they made enough money to buy a real house. After that, the apartment would be rented out to a staff member. This had some advantages and disadvantages:

Advantages:

First: The rent was usually very cheap, and included all utilities.

Second: Most of the apartments were big and nice.

Third: No commute.

Fourth: Free tours for friends.

The disadvantages:

First: You were responsible for being sober enough to answer the phones at night. And all the other times you were there.

Second: You were always accountable for the security of the place.

Third: You usually ended up doing all the oddball chores; like washing cars, windows, and vacuuming.

Fourth: You usually had to work all the evening visitations, and you worked weekends.

For two years I lived under a funeral home in its two-room dungeon. Fred the cat and I shared the place with spiders. Really big spiders.

I killed so many great, big fucking spiders living underground I want to tell you about it. When you step down on a spider to squish it, and your foot lifts up, that's a big spider. Many nights I would be sitting in my 8' by 8' concrete, rock, and dirt dungeon, having a toke, playing guitar and watching TV and out from the rocks would come two or three of these big boys. I kept a sharp eye and killed hundreds. They were aggressive spiders and they bit me. They knew that I was the enemy. Many mornings I would wake up with fresh spider bites on my arms. My cat was afraid of them. I was glad to move.

When I did move I moved upstairs into the old owner's quarters. The little old lady who had lived there for years had died. That was the quickest house call I ever made and the last time I was pissed on.

I lived in another funeral home once. This one had a big elevator that we used to move the bodies and caskets with. I shared the 3rd floor with the preparation room. I used to back my Harley into the elevator down in the basement, push the button, start it up and ride it into my living room. This was great! Many Saturday mornings were spent waxing my bike and watching the Wild, Wild West.

Another 15 Minutes of Fame

It is a Sunday afternoon and I'm in-between shifts. I'm home, my white shirt and tie still on, and I am sitting on my porch, with my feet up playing my guitar. A guy drives up the street, stops, gets out and takes my picture. There I am again! "On the Cover of the Rolling Stone". Well, not quite, but once again my smiling face was front and center in the local paper.

A Hole You Throw Money Into

Did you know that inside almost every grave dug within the past 30 years there is a concrete box? Sometimes that box costs more than the casket. It's called a grave liner, and it really has a job to do. The cemetery officials and undertakers will tell you, "It's for the protection of the deceased." This is true. It holds the weight of the world from collapsing into casket and getting mom's dress dirty. If you have ever been to the old section of an old cemetery you might have noticed sunken graves and tombstones, leaning like the tower of Pisa. These are graves that either had old wooden grave liners or none at all.

Mother Earth has now dropped in and is getting to know the person personally. The dip in the grass proves this. And it is a pain in the ass for the cemetery. It's hard to mow, and it looks macabre. Plus, if the headstone falls over, the cemetery usually has to pay to have it replaced.

They don't like doing that.

Nowadays, it is required by almost every cemetery for the casket to be placed into a grave liner. This is, in my opinion, more for the protection of the cemetery than for the protection of the body. But, what do I know? If you believe in ashes to ashes, dust to dust, who cares? A casket and a grave liner will only slow down the process. Once mama's in the hole, who will see her? Don't go and buy a $5000 hermetically-sealed, gold-colored grave vault, unless you want to. A simple grave liner will do the trick. There is a lot of profit in grave vaults, my friends.

One day a bunch of punks from out of town came in and destroyed the cemetery. They vandalized the hell out of it. Many headstones were knocked over and broken. Thousands of dollars of damage was done. They called themselves the Nail in the Coffin Gang. They all got caught. All of them were minors. And all spent some time in jail. The local cops didn't check them very close, because they locked up a girl with the rest of the gang of boys. They didn't figure it out for days, that she was a he. It truly is a mixed-up, muddled-up, shook-up world. Isn't it?

There is a lot of money in holes in the ground. I have buried enough diamonds and gold that easily could have fed half the starving folks in Ethiopia. I have closed the lid on hundreds of expensive watches, rings, necklaces, cash money, and pictures, and all kinds of memorabilia and watched it disappear down that hole.

I'm all for burying anything with anybody. It's your choice, baby.

We buried some guy one time and left his watch on. The son called up, pissed off, the next day. "It was my father's Rolex, and I want it back," he said. "OK, no problem." We called up the cemetery and made an appointment to re-open the grave. The next day we went out. With the son standing by we watched as the casket came back from the great beyond. I unlocked the lid of the casket, reached in and slid off his daddy's watch and gave it back to the man. It was a Timex.

My grandmother gave me my grandfather's watch after he died. Since his wrist was much larger than mine, my old girlfriend took it and said she would replace the watchband. It was a Rolex. That was the last time I ever saw my grandfather's watch.

When a family member asks me to do something, I do it. When they say bury mom with $10,000 worth of jewels, however, I'll ask a few questions. "Isn't there anyone in the family that would like to have it to keep as a memento?" I'll ask. This has started many family fights and in the end, if I have to (and I have) I'll bring your bad ass back up.

Still Single After All These Years

A woman came in and made funeral arrangements with me for her aunt. Her aunt had never been married. When I asked for the names of the pallbearers, she named only women. She told me what her aunt had told her; since no man had taken her out while she was alive, no man is going to take her out when she is dead. The ladies did a superb job.

The Next Day

I had a guy and his wife come in to make prearrangements. He told me he was going under the knife the next day and the odds were that he wasn't going to make it. He had never been in a funeral home in his life and wanted the *full* tour. "Sure, okay," I said.

I started them off at ground zero, the control center. Our command center was a big room with 4 desks, 4 phones, a copier, and a 4'by 8' sheet of glass mounted on the wall. Behind the sheet of glass was a white sheet. On the board was a grid of sorts which listed the names of our guests. We would have sometimes upward of 70 guests at any one time, and several had places to be. This took the old boy back a bit.

It was shocking for the outsider, but it kept us on track, and on time, and it worked.

I introduced them to the boss and staff. We walked into the selection room and I explained the joys and wonders of each type of casket we had in stock. We went into the preparation room, which was empty at that time, and I showed him all the secret stuff, and how it worked. We went downstairs and I showed them the refrigerators, where we kept our clients in climate-controlled comfort. They saw the crematories and learned how they worked.

They saw the funeral cars, and he sat behind the wheel of the hearse. He left that day a very happy man. The next day I brought him back.

Those Little Tubes

New caskets are like new cars. You can buy them plain or with all the whistles and bells. Caskets can be ordered with special interiors, custom handles and special paint. You can get many with adjustable beds (not like the kind advertised on TV, but close). Quite a few come available with a memorial tube. This tube of plastic holds the secret information about the dead person. The information is written on a scroll of sacred parchment, which is then rolled up and placed inside this special tube, which is then screwed inside the foot end of the casket. This will come in damn handy in the year 2510 if they need to dig up the casket. And it does.

The Mississippi River flooded a cemetery one time and when it left, it left caskets in trees and headstones and caskets scattered all over the place. It was a real live, dead, jigsaw puzzle.

And that is why they have those little tubes.

In America we are bombarded by choices. The funeral industry isn't any different. We give you so many choices some people can't make up their minds. Sometimes it takes a week for a family to come to grips with the reality of death, and give us the go-ahead to either cook mom or bury her. I've had families that couldn't decide which casket they wanted. Some have left the place, went home and got another relative to help decide. Some folks are really picky about our caskets. They want the blue casket, but with a pink interior, ours is white, or visa-versa.

Don't worry; we will keep your mom company for a week until a family member finally decides. "Say Mr. Undertaker. We sure do like that blue box ya got. Can we get it with the pink lining just like that other casket you got over there? It sure would match mamma's dress. And we would like to see ma tonight." "Yes," I usually say "we can do that."

Sometimes we can't. We can custom order just about anything you want, but sometimes we can't make it happen overnight.

Whose Clothes are Those?

When you work for a large funeral parlor, one that handles thousands of dead people each year, you are continually acquiring a large number of their personal assets. I'm not talking about diamonds and watches, or anything that is valuable. I'm talking about dentures, diapers, get-well cards, slippers and used clothes.

Most funeral homes keep a written inventory of all these items, and they keep them in a sack that has the dead guy's name on it. A typical list from a hospital might read; dentures, upper and lowers, one pair of pants, pair of underwear, cards; belt, a pair of socks, a T-shirt, and a pair of tennis shoes. We were constantly juggling 60 to 80 bags of this shit.

After a few years went by we would have sometimes hundreds of bags of bras and panties, shoes and socks and they would take up quite a lot of space. If only we could sell the stuff, we would really have had it made.

I dare say that if we were ever to throw out a bag of old clothes, that particular family would come wandering in the next day and ask for it.

It was really funny to watch a family, after they had signed for the bag of personal effects and while they were still in the lobby, tear into that bag, then gasp and gag after pulling out a piss-soaked pair of pants with dear old dads shitty underwear attached. Some funeral homes, to avoid this, will have these clothes laundered for the family. We didn't.

Sometimes there would be some really good stuff: a nice coat, a new pair of pants, a leather jacket, a good pair of boots, a new belt, maybe a cool T-shirt. If you ask most folks, "Hey, would you want a cool leather jacket?" most would say "Hell, yes!" If they ask "where did you get it" and you said "Well, it came off a dead guy…" "Nooo," most would say. I know, I've asked.

Usually after about a year we would toss the stuff. I can't blame people for not wanting to come in and pick up a set of used dentures, or a bunch of bloody, stinky, old clothes. We don't want them either. It's just part of the job.

We brought home a fellow once who had died and the hospital hadn't even bothered to remove the medical halo someone had screwed into his head. This piece of equipment must have cost thousands, and was literally screwed into his head at several points. We took it off his head and no one ever claimed it. It was cool.

One time we had a t-shirt we took off a guy who had been shot with a shot gun at close range. We washed it in the washing machine 20 times and it finally came out clean. It looked pretty cool to see the gunshot pattern. I grabbed a new pair of boots that we were going to throw out once, and wore them for many years.

I have heard of stories of families, who have gone to the funeral home to pick up the personal belongings of dear old dad, and have actually picked up personal body parts, of dear old dad. That's what we call a mix-up.

Halloween

We used to have a couple of fake legs lying around. When we would hire someone new, like a new office girl, we would stick one of them, dressed in pants, a sock and a shoe, and leave it under one of the cars in the basement. Once we left it dangling out of the end of the crematory. Then we would call up and ask her to come downstairs.

Halloween is a great time to be an undertaker. Especially if you were me.

Somehow I had acquired two glass eyes, which I imagine I got from two dead folks and I kept them in my desk drawer. Glass eyes are not round, like I had imagined, but kind of convex shaped. I would put one in my mouth and go show the office girls. One was blue and the other brown. Very clear looking, and very genuine.

One Halloween, I had my cousin ride down to the office on his bike. We went into the preparation room and lay down, and a co-worker friend of mine waxed an eye onto the middle of his forehead, and one onto mine. He did a really nice job. They looked cool! We had third eyes! Very cool! Very subtle.

Off we rode to the bar on our bikes. People would look at us for a while, and then notice our third eye, and say, "Cool, man! Real cool." I think we even won a prize. I remember we rode to a fancy Indian restaurant and had some spicy food. It made us sweat and the whole wax job slipped off our foreheads. We could just wipe off our foreheads and stick it back on. That was big fun.

Another year, it was Halloween and I needed a costume. I wanted to go as a big fat biker. As I was a big fat biker, the only thing I lacked to complete the ensemble was long hair and a beard.

After a funeral one afternoon I was driving back to the funeral home. On the way I passed a costume shop. Boy,

I whipped around, parked the hearse, went in and bought a longhaired black wig with a matching long beard. I walked back out, got behind the wheel, put them on, and drove off. People did a double take of my ass as I drove along or sat at traffic lights, making my way home. Some people would laugh, some would be disgusted.

Traveling

I stopped by a couple of funeral homes in Warsaw, Poland. In the first one, the lady didn't speak any English, (can you imagine?) so I left. I only remember it having about 20 tropical fish tanks in its office.

In the second one the manager spoke a little English. It was a big place that handled 500 or so deaths a year. They had a staff of 14, and they didn't look too overworked to me. The man said that embalming and cremation are done in Poland, but not to the extent that we do it in America. I didn't get to go behind the big door where the real action is, so I can't comment on how they do what they do.

One thing I noticed is that most funeral homes looked like little shit holes on the outside. Most were buried in the middle of an ugly concrete building. None of the ones I saw in Warsaw, Poland, or Moscow, Russia looked like a nice proper, clean, respectful, American funeral home. The insides of these funeral homes weren't much better. None of them had chapels, as everybody has the funeral at the church. For any reception or post-funeral parties, they usually went to someone's house.

In Amsterdam, Holland, there is a funeral home which was right inside a hospital, next to an eye doctor. I had to check that out. I was really high at the time, and they didn't speak any English so the whole affair took a few minutes. I walked around the lobby and looked in the chapel. The place was very nice.

When I was fresh out of mortuary school, I had an attitude, and a Harley, and I wanted to go to work overseas as a mortician with the armed services. I thought it would be cool to live in France or Germany or England and embalm unfortunate Americans.

I sent in the paperwork, but alas, I was not needed. It would have been a great job. Working in the Graves Registry I would have been paid as a GS11; good money. They would ship your car or bike, maybe both, right to your house, wherever it was, and pay your rent. It was too good to be true. I did the next best thing.

When I rode my motorcycle through Germany I stopped at bed and breakfast for a few days once.
There was an American staying there who knew the area well. When I told him of this old dream, he said: "Why, the US Army base is right over the hill. Give them a call." So I did. I spoke to the head honcho who, unfortunately, told me I still wasn't needed.

Later, during the Desert Storm war years the army had called up the national funeral directors association and had put together a list of all embalmers who had a passport and who would be willing to go. My name was on that list, as were thousands of others. Thank god, only a few were needed.

A Captain Goes Down With his Ship

One time three of us responded to a unique house/tug boat death call. A captain had died in his boat, and they needed us. We were, at the same time, needed at a funeral. Luckily, it was close by. We took the coach and the suburban to the lakeside dock. We parked the cars, grabbed the cot, and all of us went out to the boat. It was big, dirty, and looked very old. Two of us went down inside while the third man waited on the dock, guarding the cot. We followed the first mate, who was the dead captain's wife, down through the galley, and then down steep narrow stairs to a bedroom deep inside. We arrived at a bedroom no bigger than a closet, and in the middle of it was a very big dead man. We wrapped him up in a sheet and lifted him up into our arms and made way for sunlight. The halls and stairs of this boat were not made for two guys to carry out a third guy. I remember the wife saying over and over, "Be careful with him. CAREFUL. Don't bump his head."

Jesus H. Christ! The boat was rocking, and we were banging around bumping into everything and anything, just trying to keep our balance. We were knocking things over and banging the dead captain off the walls of his ship as we made our way out. We had a hell of a time just getting him up onto the deck. We had to slide him up the five stairs and out the hatch onto the deck. The gangplank leading from the boat to the dock was a plank of wood about 4 feet long. It was not made for two men carrying a third one. We had to jump for it. We jumped at the same time onto the dock and dropped that dead old captain onto that cot like he was a ten-ton sack of potatoes. If the third guy was not holding the cot securely, all three of us would have gotten wet. That would have made the papers. After the drama was over, the two boys went to their funeral, and I went back and made arrangements with the wife. I asked her if she and her husband ever took the boat anywhere. She said, "The only place this boat ever went was down."

Aprils Fool's Day

On Aprils Fool's Day funeral homes get the funniest phone calls. People call us and ask if we have, or can they talk to, Myra Mains. I honestly have had at least 20 people call me and ask this. The phone call usually goes something like this:

"Hello, Fred's Final Act Funeral Home. May I help you?"

"Yes. I would like to speak to Myra Mains, please."

"I'm sorry sir; there is no Myra Mains here."

"There has to be. I have a message, she just called me."

"No sir, you have been the victim of an Aprils Fool's prank." I explain.

"Why, what do you mean?" they inquire.

"Well sir, look here, you have called a funeral home. Is that right?"

"Yes" they agree.

"And you have asked for Myra Mains, is that correct?"

"Yes" they say impatiently.

"Say that name again, slowly." As they repeat it, and come to understand what the hell they are saying, some will laugh, while others will yell and swear and slam down the phone.

If I got the chance, I would ask if they would like to get back at that person. If they said yes, I would give them a number for their friend to call: 1-800 fat lady. That would connect whomever to some sexy fat lady who liked talking dirty.

Funeral homes get prank calls too. You get used to catching these with time and experience. That saves you a lot of time and trouble. I heard a story of two undertakers driving around for hours in the middle of the night looking for some non-existent address to pick up some non-existent dead guy. They didn't listen for the clues. Someone had called in a fake death call on these guys.

Ha-ha to them.

A kid once called the funeral home and I answered. He sounded about 12 and he said that his friend was dead, and would I come and pick him up. I could hear his buddies laughing in the background. I asked for the address and when he stuttered I knew, I had a fish on the line. So, I let out more line.

"Well, I'm very sorry about your friend. How did he pass away"? I asked.

"Umm…" he said.

"Was it an accident?" I asked.

"Yes! Yes it was," he said.

"Oh, have you called the police?" I asked.

"No" he said.

"What's the name of his doctor?" I asked.

"Ummm, well, ummm" he stumbled.

"He didn't have a doctor?" I asked.

"No, he didn't. He just dropped dead, just now on the couch," he said.

"What was the address again?" I asked.

"Well, I don't know, I don't live here," he said.

"No problem. I'll have the police trace the line, right now and they will be right there." I said. Click went the phone. Fool me once, the joke is on you; fool me twice and the joke is on me.

Funeral for a Fly

I went on a house call with a co-worker one time. It was quite far away from town, and the house was at the end of a long drive. The whole family was there. Their mom was dead on the couch, covered with a sheet. It was a very hot day, and she had begun to smell. We went over to take a peek before going back out to get the cot. I pulled back the sheet to take a look. Her eyes were open, dry and looking straight at me, her mouth an open, gaping hole. Immediately, two huge, I mean really big, flies flew out from her mouth. I jumped back, and the family members who were standing behind me just about fainted. I quickly replaced the sheet. We went out, got the cot, put her on it and took her back to the van. I went back in and made the arrangements and after that, we took off. Another fly escaped from the mouth of doom on the way back and it was buzzing all around us. We stopped and opened up all the doors and windows we could. It still took a while to get that little fucker out.

Another time, at another place, I was handling a visitation. This time a husband had lost his wife. He was in the chapel with her and I was standing by outside the door. It was a beautiful hot sunny day. He came out and said to me a fly had just flown out of her nose. I apologized all over myself and said I would take care of it. Other than that, what else could I do?

Undertakers hate flies. When people stand in our doorway holding the doors wide open waiting 15 minutes for mom to finish walking across the parking lot, we just flinch. I know flies can smell death. And they love funeral homes, which use all kinds of insecticides to kill every flying insect we can, but the bastards still get in. To try to stop the problem of flies keeping house in mom's nose, undertakers will sometimes cover the open casket with a see-through cloth. Otherwise, we use small cotton balls, saturated with chemicals and we stick them up the dead people's noses. But, we must stick the cotton way up there so no one can see it. Which leaves for the fly, no matter how smelly, a perfect little nostril nursery.

I have watched flies and bugs fly around during funerals many times. It's very funny to be in the back of the chapel and watch a fly dive-bomb the preacher. Some preachers get right after the critter and try to kill it during their sermon. Other preachers are so cool, they pay it no attention. When I have noticed a fly or a bug crawling on the casket I know that others have seen it too. People start to follow the fly around the room with their eyes and forget about the funeral and the preaching. The fly, or June bug, as was one bug I remember, is now the center of attention. Believe me, it is the center of attention when it lands on mammas head and starts crawling around on mamma's face. Everybody in the fucking chapel is looking at that bug crapping on mom, and I'm in the back trying like hell to get the attention of the preacher to have him wave it away. Some preachers are oblivious to the world and me and continue with their sermon lost in the spotlight, and blind to their surroundings. Usually someone, either from the family or sitting close will step forward to try and swat it away. This is usually impossible as well, but also funny to watch. I've always wanted to see someone using a bible, smash a fly onto a casket.

Remember, we're all God's little creatures.

Here is my idea; a bug zapping device built into a casket which cremates or, as I like to use the word, evaporates, any bug when they enter into its airspace. It would have to use stealth technology and be very quiet as it might not be considered respectful to be frying flies at a funeral.

These Things I So Remember

I remember hearing these special phrases coming from the mouths of the undertakers:

Blessed are those who play dominoes
Spectacle, testicle, wallet and watch

Toast em' and toss em', burn em' and box em', shake em and bake em'.

I just thought you should know.

After Lunch

One time after lunch, my partner and I drove up to a house to pick up the dead. The family, plus a few of the neighbors were standing outside. Old Joe, an uncle to one of them, was inside on the bed, they said. They told us that the coroners had just left as well. They also said it smelled real bad and there were lots of cats inside. We walked up and went inside. Man o' Man! Jesus fucking Christ! They weren't kidding. This old boy had about 15 cats, and they all had fleas. It stunk! There wasn't a window open for the cats to come and go. He had piled up his garbage against the back door, but he hadn't taken it out, for what looked like months. Garbage sacks extended from the back kitchen door out into the kitchen, many of which had been torn open. The kitchen motif was cat shit and garbage.

The most unusual thing I noticed was how the carpet seemed to move. There must have been millions of fleas living there. We went to the bedroom, and there he was, dead on the bed. The bed had white sheets but they were black with fleas. We had seen enough. We went back outside, spoke with the family who then left, and brought our cot back inside the house. Once inside we hustled our asses off; we had him in a plastic sheet wrapped up and taped tight faster than an unexpected fart, and out the door we went. We looked cool, calm, and collected as we walked away from that house to the van with fleas jumping all over us and the cot. We drove two blocks, and parked in an alley. We both jumped out and lifted our pants, checking our legs for fleas. My buddy had fleas all over. I couldn't find any. The next day, he showed me his legs, both were covered with bites. I didn't have one; it must be the coffee.

One for All

We used to handle a lot of funerals for a particular religious group. When one would die they would all use the same casket. We kept it on a shelf for them. We would go get the body, and they would follow us to the funeral home and do the rest. The body would be wrapped in a sheet and placed in their nice oak casket. Next, we would drive it to the mosque. They would carry it to the door, where we would all kick off our shoes, and carry it inside. Then, they would have their service and we would wait outside. After the service, off to the cemetery we would go. They used one cemetery, and they had purchased quite a bit of land there, in advance, so they could be buried facing Mecca. This was a different direction than most graves face, which is to the east. For the second coming of Christ, they say. Anyway, after their graveside service, they lifted Mohamed from the casket and into the grave he went. No casket and no grave liner were ever used. Then they all grabbed shovels and filled in the grave. Nice and simple. After it was all said and done, they paid us in cash (they always paid us in cash); we would put the casket back in the hearse, and then back on its shelf until the next time.

What Church Do You Attend?

In Havana, Cuba, I became interested in checking out old churches. They have a church where you can look through the floor and see caskets buried below. I took pictures. This idea of burying folks in the church was more common than I thought.

It seemed that to be closer to God, people wanted to be buried inside the church. However, once the church was filled they had to bury you outside in the graveyard, beside the church. God's acre, it was called. If you were rich and important the church might make an exception, for a small donation, and dig up the floor and bury you alongside older, noble dead folks. You will find this all over Europe. I heard a story that to cover the smell from all these rotting important dead people underfoot, churches began to use incense. If you had the money, some folks used sarcophaguses made from limestone for keeping the smell down.

The sarcophaguses of some of the Russian czars in St. Petersburg, and Moscow, Russia, are very cool to check out.

In Vienna, Austria, the Habsburgs, a ruling family of a thousand years, have their hearts in urns, decorating a room in their palace. You can go and take a look. I did.

Churches are fascinating places to visit. Really Russian in Russia, Golden in Thailand, Inspirational in India and Amazing in Asia. Their churches outshine our American churches. I can't say which country had the most far-out church, as all were gigantic, decorated with marble, granite, gold, and silver. I can say that while I saw many people in many countries living in mud shacks, they sure had some fancy churches to go to. I heard that in Europe it was a law that nothing could be built taller than the church. So they built them big. Most churches could be seen for miles.

In Moscow, Russia, I wandered though an unbelievable church. It's called Christ the Savior. They had just rebuilt it, and it was ready for service. Remember, religion was allowed in Russia, and then banned, for a couple of generations. Stalin had destroyed this church many years ago and was going to instead have a statue of himself built on this holy spot. It was supposed to be as tall as the Empire State Building. But, shit happens; the ground was swampy, old Joseph died, and the statue was never built. Instead, they built a swimming pool. But, times change, and religion is back in vogue in Russia, and so they rebuilt this church right down to the last detail. It was amazing! I couldn't believe that Joseph would have ever torn it down were it not for the gold. Someone got a lot of gold. But what the hell do I know.

I know a man who swam in the pool.

I was amazed at the amount of time and money toil and sacrifice that went into building these churches. How many people died working on them is a mystery. But there they stand. Many, I noticed, now stand empty.

Churches are used as Art Galleries in Amsterdam, Holland. It's a great use for the unused buildings. In America, churches are turned into houses.

Trade Business

When your granny dies in the specialty hospital that was trying to save her 800 miles away from her hometown, who goes and gets her? How does she get back home? Well, after we get the first call from a family, we call up a local funeral home in the designated city. We, in the industry, call it, a trade call, and it is done everywhere. The funeral home we call does most of the work; they pick up the body, and they embalm it. Then we go and get it.

All funeral homes are supposed to help out each other. It's called professional courtesy. I used to work at a funeral home in a big city that did a lot of trade work for the smaller firms in the area.

The phone would ring at 0400 hours and it would be Old Ma, from Ma and Pa's Funeral Home. She would ask us to please pick up Mr. Cheese Pizza for them, and deliver.

One funeral home we made calls for had nice young girls living in the upstairs apartment. Their job was to answer the phones at night, and maybe help with the evening visitations. I used to work with this old man who loved to go with me if we had a call for this funeral home. He would go to the door and I would drive around back. The girls knew we would be showing up and would almost always answer the door in their teddies. This would really get the old man going. He would be so excited that he couldn't sit still. I think the girls loved it too.

We had a couple of girls living in an upstairs apartment at a funeral home I worked for. One weighed 340+ pounds. The other one weighed a little less. The big girl had a white Volkswagen Beetle convertible. Watching her squeeze herself in and out of that car was quite a sight. The car would give a sigh of relief when she got out and groan when she got in.

I probably left the door to the preparation room of that funeral home open one night because the next morning somebody or something had eaten the end of someone's nose off. These girls had cats. We fixed that.

Smoke Signals

We all know that smoking causes death. But I didn't know that smoking could lead you to death.
One day we were sitting around the office, waiting for someone to die, and the phone rang. Someone died. We now had to go and pick up this dead guy from his 10th floor apt. My partner and I drove to one of those low-income apartment buildings on the edge of the slums, and

parked in front. We were in an unmarked suburban. We rolled the cot into the lobby and up to the elevator. Melted into the linoleum floor from the front door to the elevator were burnt cigarette butts. This mosaic style of artwork had taken a long time to create. The elevator had hundreds, maybe more. Lo and Behold! When we got off on the 10th floor, the trail continued. It lead us right to the door we were going to. We knocked, and we were greeted by someone from social services. When we went in, the trail concluded. There, in a lounge chair, surrounded by half-finished cigarettes, with melted cigarette butts stuck to the floor, sat our (no longer) smoking gun. The chair had so many burns in it it's a wonder it didn't ever catch fire. The entire floor of his low-rent, federally-subsidized, low-income apartment, was one big ashtray.

But Seriously

I picked up a dead guy with a porn collection that would make a porn collector jealous. This fellow had all the inflatable dolls and strap-on devices known to man. I met the family downstairs after we had him out of his place and forewarned them about what to expect. They knew.

A mountain climbing friend of mine told me a story once, when I was in England. He was climbing up a cliff, somewhere in Scotland I think. It was the straight up and down kind of cliff where you hold on with your nose, toes and fingertips.

Well as this chap was climbing up, having a great old time, there was a noise from above. My friend turned and looked, and watched a fellow from above him fall away and drop to his death. As this doomed fellow passed my friend, he said: "What the fuck..." He didn't yell it or even yell out. That was all he said. And that was the last time my friend went rock climbing there.

Funerals are supposed to be serious events. And they are. However, some ministers are sometimes much too serious. If I knew the minister well, I would liven up these occasions as they did their service. I would stand in the back, out of sight by everyone but him, and begin to try and make him laugh. I would make faces or laugh, quietly of course, because, after all, I AM the undertaker. I would pretend to pick my nose, scratch myself or juggle stuff to distract him into mixing up his service or smile, when the moment really didn't call for a smile, but a serious look of contemplation, as he reflected on the life of Mr. Ed. Some would get really confused and mad and have to start over. Others would ignore me, and I caught hell a few times too. A few folks attending the service have caught me. One old lady caught me with two pencils up my nose. I was trying to get a smile out of an old minister. She looked at me with so much disgust; I thought she was going to call my boss. But she didn't.

The Wrong Song

It's really wonderful when a family brings me a taped cassette with the music to play at the funeral. This makes it much easier for me. No songs to look up and no musicians to find to play the songs that have been requested. Sometimes that can really be a bitch. People can come up with the most unusual songs. I have to find the sheet music with the song, and then someone who knows how to play it. With taped music, I just push a few buttons and away we go.

The tape, which usually shows up one minute before the service starts, is put in the machine side A up, as requested. The service begins. I get the cue from the minister for music and I push play and more often that not this is what happens: the song starts in the middle, or worse yet, nothing happens. Total silence. Better yet, and this has happened too, it's the wrong tape altogether. I am playing heavy rock and roll, anti-Christ music for a holier-than-thou dead person. Either way, immediately everybody knows that there has been a fuck up, and it's my fault, even when it's not. When you are an undertaker however, everything is your fault, when something goes wrong during a funeral.

My Fault

A lady yelled at me once during a rainy graveside service for not having enough umbrellas at the cemetery. We had brought all we had (10 big ones), which wasn't enough. She didn't have one and subsequently got soaked. After I explained I was sorry we didn't have another umbrella for her, I felt like adding, "My mother taught me not to go out in the rain without an umbrella." But I didn't.

Umbrellas are a great item for a rainy graveside service. It looks good to be seen giving the last one, the one you have saved for yourself, to some middle-aged lady. But how many should a funeral home have? 25 or 50 umbrellas? Maybe funeral homes should hire people to stand around with umbrellas at rainy graveside funerals to keep the stupid people who don't bring one dry. If it just looks like it will rain, bring an umbrella. If you plan to stand out in the cold rain, wear a coat; it's plain and simple.

It's also my fault that the graveside isn't completely free of snow and ice. It doesn't matter that it is five below zero, and it's snowing and blowing to the beat the band.

It's amazing to me how tough some old folks are. I have stood at many cemeteries. The wind is just about to blow trees over, it's cold and the snow is falling fast or the rain is coming down in buckets and there you stand, tall, proud and impervious to the weather. And you stand, and stand, and stand. Over an hour can easily go by. I am wearing a thick winter coat, boots, gloves, and I am freezing my ass off and there you stand. You're Incredible.

Many times, when it is chilly at the cemetery, I'll place my really warm black leather trench coat over the shoulders of the one who needs it the most. This looks good. Who cares if I have a cold for a week because of it?

Wet Spot

A long time ago, when I was a kid in a suit, young, dumb, and full of cum as they say, I was working the night shift at the funeral home, alone. My job was to load and unload the crematories. We had a special cart we used for carrying the bodies around on. It was called Parker, and I would load a body onto Parker and push it to the crematory and slide in the body.

Parker was made of wood and consisted of two parts; a cart, which sloped downward at the handle end, and a long slider board onto which we put the bodies. You would drop the body from the cooler shelf onto the cart and roll it to the crematory. Then you open the door and slide the long board with the body on it into the retort and quickly pull the board back out. It worked great and it was relatively easy to use unless you had a fat one.

It was sometime during the early evening twilight hours and I had just barely loaded a big fat guy into a very hot crematory when soon afterwards as I was making up some urns, the crematory began making all kinds of funny noises. It sounded like it was burping, and farting. I didn't know what the hell was happening, so I didn't do anything. The front doorbell all of a sudden began to ring incessantly so I took off my work coat and gloves and went upstairs to answer it. A guy was standing there, wide-eyed and screaming: "Your building is on fire!!! Your building is on FIRE!!!" "What! No it isn't," I said, but I walked out into the street and looked up where he was pointing. Out from the chimney, which was about 40 feet tall, blew a 20-foot ball of flame, with lots of black smoke billowing from it. "Thanks" I said to the guy, and I ran back inside. I turned off the crematory, and waited. Just then the back door bell rang. I answered it and again was told that the building is on fire! I looked up saw, no flames, but lots of black smoke. Pretty soon that stopped and it was barely smoking. "Thank you" I said, shut the door and I went back to work getting an urn ready. Sure enough, a couple minutes later I heard the siren of a fire truck, and it was getting closer. I walked outside when I knew from the sound that it was close, to greet it. Around the corner, with two drivers, came a big hook and ladder fire truck. The fire marshal didn't even get out. I met him in the street. "Where's the fire?" He asks me. I said there wasn't any fire, I had just got a body too hot, and it kind of smoked up a bit. "God damn it" he said "I wish they had looked to see where the flames were coming from before they called us." "Sorry" I said." No problem," he said, and off they drove. I went back and looked in the retort. The fat old fellow had rendered out, and turned to grease. This is what had caught fire. When I turned off the retort that had cut the gas off and that had put out the fire. He, however, continued for a while to turn into grease and I cleaned up his lovely greasy mess. He overfilled a four gallon grease pan, and left a very large, very hot, wet spot on the floor.

I named my bar the wet spot.

The Writing's on the Tombstone

I like selling headstones. That's where you can really find out what kind of person the dead person was. Some of the epitaphs folks have used have really said it all. There are books about this. Some folks have traveled the world writing this stuff down.

I was in a bar once and there was a sign from God on the back bar of a tombstone with some writing on it. My professional curiosity got the best of me and I ask to read it. It said:

> And when I'm gone and in my grave
> No more pussy will I crave,
> And on my tombstone shall be written:
> I've had my share, and I ain't shitting.
> When I die, bury me deep.
> Make it simple, and make it cheap.
> Upon my tombstone I want wrote:
> Millions of drinks have gone down my throat.
> And if you should pass by where I lie,
> Piss on me. I'm always dry.

I liked that one.

I remember another epitaph I engraved for a family on an urn. It was a quote from a Beatles' song. "The love you take is equal to the love you make." I thought that was nice.

I have fulfilled the requests for ships, golf clubs, lighting bolts, motorcycles, cars, horses, mountains, and all kinds of stuff to be carved on tombstones. What do you want on your tombstone?

Just Waiting Around

People call us up all the time to tell us mom is just about dead, so we will be calling you again very soon. So we wait and wait. It's always these people that live for months.

I wish these people wouldn't call us until the death occurred. Many times, as I was just about to go somewhere to do something fun, the phone would ring. Now, because of this 'pending death call' I have just received, I have stayed home and missed out on all kinds of sex, drugs and rock and roll, waiting for a phone call that doesn't come.

We are on call 24 hours, 7 days a week. We have pagers, answering services, cell phones and computers to make our lives more mobile. And it does. And yet, that pending death call still catches me off guard.

Imagine you have concert tickets for tonight and you get this type of phone call. You are screwed if you go to the concert, and you're screwed if you don't. If you don't go, the phone won't ring, and you will have missed a rare concert and you will be pissed. If you go, right after that second joint, and before the concert starts, the pager will ring and you and your date will have to leave, and you are pissed. I know.

I have been interrupted by my pager having a really good time at some really good parties. Two minutes later off I go, chewing on a piece of gum.

I always carry gum. Most of the undertakers I knew always carried some kind of mouthwash; mints or gum too. I have picked up my share of dead people while I was drunk. Many times the family is also drunk and we all have a toast. I've never, however, been too drunk to do my job respectfully. Sometimes, no matter what you're doing or where you are, you just have to go. They won't come to you.

I received a phone call one Saturday night around11:00 pm about someone who had died at home. They needed us, the smoother movers. I called up my co-worker friend and subsequently ruined his night. I told him I needed his help and he told me he was currently completely covered in chocolate sauce. "Well, hurry up." I said. When he showed up his white shirt looked like it was stuck on. That was classic. I sure miss that guy. He died a year later. Undertakers die too.

Chicken

One of the places I worked was busy enough that we really kept the midnight fires burning all night long. We were busy enough to kept the midnight fires burning all day long too. We popped in, and swept out, lots of folks. One Saturday morning, we loaded up all the retorts and left to pick up more customers. We were kept busy all that day and only in the afternoon, when I went to check on things in the basement, did I realize that I had forgotten to actually start up one crematory. Baked chicken was what I smelled when I pushed open the garage door. When I opened up the retort door a little to see, I saw a golden-brown, glistening, baked to perfection body. That was sick. But, now ya know, 400 degrees for 7 hours; perfect, give or take a few.

I had only pushed the preheat button, starting the sequence which only warmed the oven up. I hit the main burner switch and went to lunch.

Very Nasty

The town is called Varanasi. It is in India. I have never been there, but I got close. It is the holiest of holy cities when it comes to being cremated. In India, when you gotta go, it's the place to be.

I tried to get there from Agra, India, where I had been checking out the Taj Mahal. The Taj Mahal, everybody said, is the coolest place to be staying if you're dead, so I had to see it. It is amazing. The Taj sits alongside and high-up on a bank of the Yamuna River. Tourists were gathering at a vista point inside the grounds and were looking out over the river. I walked up and had a look and there in the distance was a dog eating away on what looked like a body. That was amazing. I would have stayed and lingered but it was time to catch the train.

I was relying on the good old Indian railroad system to bring me safely into Varanasi in the wee hours of the following morning which would have given me 10 hours to witness the most pure form of cremation there is. Many people, however, find it the most gruesome form of cremation and therefore are drawn to the spectacle like flies to corpses. Thanks to technology and modern mobility many more people of the faith can get to be cremated on the shores of the Ganges River in Varanasi than ever before. And guess what? Mixed in with its ancient history, tradition is now glitz, it is a tourist trap.

You can rent a seat in a boat and float by the many Ghats where the bodies are burned. Or, if you prefer you take a leisurely stroll around the Ghats maybe, walk up to the fire, if you dare, and take a closer look.

As you float along the Ganges River, watching the morning sun burn through the smoke, haze and pollution, sipping your Bloody Mary enjoying the smell of burning flesh, be sure to have your camera hidden, they don't like you taking pictures. The reason for that is out of respect. I however, heard the rest of the story.

This story came from someone who lives there and reads the local paper. In a nut shell, too many people are coming to Varanasi to be cremated. The increases in bodies lead to a huge increase in prices of the different types of wood used. Now, all of a sudden they have more body than wood to burn it.

FUCK!

No one can afford the wood so less wood is used. There's nothing better than a half-cooked cremated body. This really pisses off my friend; it's a holy ritual to be cremated, but there is nothing holy about doing a half ass job of it.

Oh yeah, if while you're still floating you feel a bump, don't look overboard. My friend also told me there are many half-baked, floating toasties also floating in the Ganges. So many that the city of Varanasi bought thousands of turtles to help eat up the problem.

My problem was that due to the train being so late, I never got to see any of this cool shit in Varanasi. I had to wait until I got to Katmandu.

When I was in Katmandu, Nepal, I went to a holy site and watched several people being cremated. The bodies were covered up completely by wood at the start, and the old fellows added wood as necessary to get the job done right. This special class of folks who do all this get to keep all the gold and whatever else they find. I also visited the local store where the families bought the items that they needed. It was busy, and I didn't need to buy anything, so I didn't stay long. The river that flowed by the Ghats was barely a creek, and the banks of it were covered with trash. There were very few tourists where I was, so I stood out. Luckily my guide was cool and he told me about some holy priests who lived in some caves up the river. They smoked pot. "Let's go" I said.

We walked up the river and turned up onto a rocky trail up to a building that was carved out of the side of a cliff. We went further up and into a cave. Inside were 5 men. One was dressed in color. They had pot, and a guitar and I had money. Twenty minutes later, by the side of a fire, in a cave, outside of Katmandu, Nepal, the head Guru of Gurus and I were getting stoned. He was playing his hand-pumped organ, and singing in Nepalese and I was playing his guitar. Man, I was high as Mt. Everest.

I never saw Mt. Everest.

Did You Seen Me on TV?

I have been on television.

There had been a car accident where a lady had pulled out in front of a big truck. It was a mess! My job was to wipe up what was left of her head that was now smeared into the highway. There was blood, brains, eyeballs, teeth, hair and bones smashed into the road. I got a bucket and some towels from the car, and as I kneeled down and wiped up the mess, a cameraman about 10 feet in front of me started filming. Well, I gave him one of those looks, like: "Turn off the fucking camera you sick fuck! Can't you see what I'm doing?" He filmed me until I was done. Later, there I was, on the 6 o'clock news with a towel full of hair kneeling down in the middle of the road.

Everybody has a video camera nowadays, and everybody is filming everybody else. Where there is a tragedy and loss of life you can bet somebody will probably have it on tape, and soon afterwards an undertaker will be there to help pick up the pieces.

We do a great job helping out where there have been a lot of deaths.

When there are plane crashes, bus accidents or bombings, and there are hundreds of dead bodies all lying about torn up and blown to pieces, we are there to do what must be done to help identify, record, and preserve all the victims. Remember Oklahoma City? A hundred and eighty seven people died. Undertakers from all around the country worked for weeks helping identify those people. How about the last couple of plane crashes? We were there as well. We're there when there is a bus accident, and 20 children are dead.

We're the ones who work all night for weeks to help restore some humanity back into the towns and families who are crushed by such a loss. These tragedies happen all the time. At each one, you will find an undertaker or maybe several doing what has to be done 24 hours a day, 7 days a week. You might, however have to look hard to find them, for it's what we do that people don't see, that make us better human beings.

Hoarders

This old man and I went to a house to pick up someone one time, and when we stopped in front of the house, all you could see was junk. There was a small thin path from the gate to the house. On both sides of the path were wheels, tires, BBQs, lawn mowers, ladders, and other kinds of shit. God and this fellow only knew what was there. Inside was no different. Again, there was only a thin path through the living room into the kitchen and on into the bedroom and over to the bathroom. Every other place in the house was occupied by mounds of newspapers, stacks of boxes of magazines, and clothes. This man must have kept every newspaper and every piece of clothing he had ever had. There were bags of garbage everywhere and it smelled. It looked like the dishes had never been washed as the sink was plumb full-up. It also seemed like they had been there a year or two. There was one chair, a TV and a TV tray.

On the bed was this dead fellow. He wasn't long dead, as a neighbor had noticed that he hadn't picked up his morning paper and called the cops. The cops had shown up and contacted his son, who had called us and was there when we arrived. But, interestingly enough, this dead fellow happened to be one tall dead fellow. We looked at each other. There was no way in hell could we get a cot in the house and through the maze to the bed, so we have to go to plan B.

Plan A is always use a cot so you don't hurt yourself carrying someone else. Plan B is used when plan A doesn't work.

We wrapped him up in a sheet and lifted him up and into our chests and walked as gracefully as we could out the bedroom door. The trails through the house were engineered by and for a vertical, thin man to navigate, not two big boys carrying that same thin guy horizontally. We were a wide load on a narrow curvy road. As we were holding him close to our hearts, and negotiating our way out we also had to lift him up and over several stacks of shit as we went out. Well, we didn't make it 10 feet when we turned a corner entering the living room from the kitchen and knocked over a lamp, and a stack of newspapers. We didn't lose our load and we got him out and onto the cot which was by the gate. The old undertaker told me in the car that hoarders like that might have ten thousand dollars in cash hidden between the stacks of newspapers. Boy, I wanted to go back, but I never did.

Big People and Small Houses

Why is it that when you go to the smallest house, you end up picking up the biggest dead guy you can imagine? In most cases he also will not be in a bed, on a couch or in a chair. Oh, no, not somewhere easy to get to and move. Oh, no, he'll be somewhere else.

I went to a house, it was a tiny trailer to be honest, and there was a 300-pound man, naked in the bathroom wedged tight between the toilet and the bathtub.

You tell me, how do you remove a 300-pound naked man, with a house full of family standing in the hall, all watching you, gracefully and respectfully from between a toilet and a tub?

   A. Use a lot of liquid soap? No, although that wouldn't have been a bad idea.

   B. We use muscle and might.

It just about killed us to get him out from between the toilet and the tub. Man, he was wedged in there tight as a drum.

There was about enough room in the bathroom for one person. Not three. We were tripping all over each other. But we draped him in the always-respectful sheet and pulled like hell. I stood in the shower. With a lot of lifting and pulling and huffing and puffing, he finally popped free and slid out onto the bathroom floor, along with a heap of shit. Now we were faced with getting him down the narrow hall, and onto the cot. The only way it would work was to gently slide him down the hall on the carpet and into the living room and then lift him onto the cot. We did it, cleaned up the bathroom floor, and everything went fine.

Talk about a way to hurt your back.

I have removed several folks from their bathrooms over the years. Some have remarkable balance and are still sitting on the toilet. They get stuck to it and I have had to pry them off.

Like Elvis, that last crap killed 'em.

Another time we were called by the medical examiners to come and pick up a body. When we arrived at the tiny apartment, the coroners showed us to a small bathroom where the bathtub was full of brown murky water. "Watch this," said one coroner, and he reached in and pulled the plug. Glug, glug, out went the brown, smelly water and rising up from the depths into view came a tiny little shriveled up old man.

It was another of those little bathrooms big enough for the one person who uses it, but not three. We lifted this wet slimy fellow out and because he was slimy, and his skin was slipping off, one fellow lost his grip, slipped, and knocked the sink off the wall. Water from the broken pipe shot all over the place and in no time we were all soaking wet. We put the body back down in the tub, and after turning off the valve below the sink next to the wall, we went back to work. We got the body on the cot and left.

The old manager of the apartment house, who had been watching us, had a fit about us breaking the sink, but oh well, shit happens. I bet if that dead fellow was looking down on us, he was laughing his ass off.

One of the best-remembered calls I ever made involved the Medical Examiner's office as well. They had been called about a dead guy found in his room. They arrived, ascertained that he had been under a doctor's care, had a poor medical history and was expected to die. They themselves were not needed in this case, as a doctor was willing to sign the death certificate. This releases them from jurisdiction as well as releases them from having to pick it up.

They could release the body to us. Boys, come and get it.

This body was on the second floor of a flophouse. Below it, on the first floor was a flop house bar.

The coroners were laughing when we showed up. The smell was awful, and the cops were gagging.

We got along with the medical examiner's office, probably better than most undertakers, because, we worked just as hard as they did. We both picked up lots of dead bodies, but they saw the worst side of death.

They never get to go to a nice little house with a little old lady, lying dead in a bed, all dressed in white. Nope, these guys saw all the real good stuff. Murders, suicides, drowning, accidents, all the stuff TV shows are made of.

When they were through, they would call us.

This guy was lying on his back in bed and was so bloated he looked like a beached blue whale ready to burst! No kidding! All he had on was white marble baggers. You know the kind of underwear your mother made you wear when you were a kid. His tongue stuck out about 5 inches and his balls sticking out from the shorts were the size of grapefruit. His arms and legs were stretched out, wide open and as tight as skin on a drum. He weighed 275 at least. You could almost see the juices dripping from the bed to the floor. The mattress was touching the floor.

It was a lovely sight.

Just lovely.

All around the bed the carpet was a sea of wet goo. I mean all around him for 10 feet! We carried our cot (while the boys from the M.E.'s office laughed) in over the slop, squish, squish, squish to his bedside. His goo was over the heels and soaking into the leather of my shoes. That night I would have to buy a new pair.

I was gagging like I had just seen a ten-day-old rotten, bloated, man lying in a sunken bed, in the middle of a ten foot pool of ooze. Can you imagine? Would you want to?

Before we even started in the room, we decided how we were going to tackle this job. We opened up one of the plastic sheets and draped it over the cot. Then we put on gloves and gowns, which we had, luckily, and, carrying the cot, went in the room. That way the wheels would not get so gooey. Then, we put the cot beside the bed and lowered it to the floor. Next, we each grabbed an edge of the bed sheet that goes over the mattress, one of us on each end of the bed, and, on the count of three, one-two-three, lifted the sheet and him over and onto the cot with a big ker-plop!

Blood, juices, and shit went flying everywhere. But, not too much on us. We had managed to drop him on the cot, so that was good. Because we had the cot prepared with a plastic sheet, we quickly wrapped him up and left the room.

That was one of the juiciest deaths I have ever had the pleasure of feeling. Thank you.

Do you want to know how they found this guy?

Some body having a drink in the bar noticed something dripping from the ceiling onto the bar.

Hey…umm, Mac. Looks like ya got a water leak...

Too Many Choices

It doesn't take long in this business to become accustomed to death.

Here is some bad luck. Once, we were asked to discreetly come to an address. We show up in our non-discreet Suburban. This turned out to be a Doctor's office. We walked into a lobby full of people and very professionally and quietly explained to the receptionist who we were. We were quickly led through the lobby, down the hall, inside a visiting room. There was a dead man in a chair. We were in a doctor's office. This poor fellow came in for a check-up and checked out. We went back outside, drove the Suburban to the back door, and grabbed our man as quiet as a mouse, and as quick as a cat.

However, each death is different and unique to any other death.

It is very sad to lose your parents or someone close. The best thing a funeral director can do, in my opinion, is listen and provide whatever the family asks.

In the old days, funeral directors told families what they could have, and couldn't have, and that was that. It all came down to how much money they wanted to spend.

Isn't it funny, how everything in life from living to dying comes down to money?

It was the funeral director's way, or no way. I don't think they would let you mix and match or tailor the services, in those old, pre-1970's days. Funeral homes offered the families choices. They used to have three or four types of funerals. Each type of service came complete with a casket, a funeral and a trip to the cemetery. The poor folks got taken care of and so did the rich. No choices, but you got what you could afford.

When I was in Havana, Cuba, I visited a funeral home and they had three choices as well.

I was glad that at our funeral home we would do anything, within reason, that a family asked.

A lady once wanted to see her husband.

Okay. I went and prepared the body for a visit. When I had the body in the visitation room, I ushered her in. She asked if she could touch him.

No problem, I said.

Then she asked, if she could hug him.

Okay.

Next she wanted to kiss him.

No problem.

Then she asked... if she could climb up and lie down next to him on the slumber bed...

"Well," I said, "I don't think that would be reasonable."

I blamed it on the lack of room for two, and the strength of the slumber bed. Slumber beds are designed to slumber, not to rumble.

Do dead people really slumber? Beats me.

I have wondered why no one has come up with a casket built for two. It's my idea. I have had several unfortunate funerals where both a husband and wife have been killed. So why not have a casket built for two?

For a small additional fee if requested, I would arrange both of you as you wished. Hell, I think it might work. I could become the owner of the first X-rated funeral home. I'd call it the Final Act Funeral Home, lasting pleasure is our policy.

Well, there might be some technical problems, and, you can bet the religious communities would be against it. There would also be some trouble moving a doublewide casket. Doorways would be a bitch, and you would need a hoist and a flatbed truck to move it. Plus you would have to buy two graves at the cemetery. It might not be illegal, but I can't say. None of these problems are insurmountable, though, and if you have the money, I've got the time.

The Beginning of the End

It was a wonderful life for many years. Many people thought I had it made; making good money, wearing nice suits, driving nice cars and living large. But, all good things got to come to an end and it almost happened to me.

I was having an after-hours party one night at my place, above the funeral home, and right after my guests left, which was around 3AM, the phone rang. They called me from a pay phone. They said there was a cop car watching the place. This wasn't good news. The place was on the second floor, and did have a glass door, to a very small patio. But, someone could, from the street, using binoculars' see into the apartment. But nothing happened and the winter passed. Sometime later a cop came up to me at the local coffee shop and said, "Hey Todd, I didn't know you smoked?" I said I didn't, and I walked back to my office.

I often ate lunch with the cops, went to the sheriff's office, and because I worked alongside them pulling bodies, they knew me and I knew them.

Along about this time in my life I was getting restless. I wanted to buy this old pop stand of a funeral home and make my mark as an owner. I was already in the process of refinancing a trailer court I owned for the down payment. I wanted the sun, the moon, and right of first refusal on the stars. The owners couldn't come to a quick agreement on that. And more time passed.

One night around midnight, there was a single car fatality and I went. I was, as usual, as I was. We got the guy from up out of the ditch and away I went. The next day I walked over to the sheriff's office to deliver the death certificate to the sheriff and get his "John Hancock" on it and again I was, as usual, as I was. When I opened the door to their office a drug dog that was sitting by the door barked. I just about jumped out of my fucking $200 shoes! Boy did those boys look at ME! I walked on over to the sheriff, sat down, and we shot the shit while he signed the certificate and then away I went.

Tick Tock.

It was late spring when the checks came. Almost $38,000, made out to ME. Shit started happening quick then. I was now interested in doing something legendary. People had been telling me stories for over 20 years about how they had wished they had gone somewhere, and done something, but life, love, kids, jobs, or money had kept them from going and now it was too late. I loved listening to the stories the vets told me, the wives, the husbands, the sons and daughters, and the stories the friends told about what they did. We would lament the "would have always wanted to do" stories.

Some people are packed and ready to go and others are leaving. I was leaving this town. "The time had come. I made my choice. Destiny is taking me on a different course." -- words from a song of mine. I was 40, I had no life; I was glued to a funeral home with no relief. No love; my old lady left me for someone else, no kids, but I now had a big bag o' money. So, I wrote a nice letter of resignation giving a thirty day notice. I moved everything into storage, and it wasn't long before I didn't even own a fucking key!

In 48 days I was in Jamaica. Then Cuba. Then England. A couple of months later I bought a fucking fast motorcycle, and I was going to go a hundred miles an hour all the way to the end. To the end of the world or around it, whichever came first.

It took two years, and I never saw the end of the world. I got close once or twice. I went around the world twice just to make sure I saw it all. And let me say, I tried to.

Thanks to the fickle finger of fate, that day when I felt its pointed finger touching me, I retired and became a traveling man; I went where people told me to go. I stayed in my tent less than 10 times. And, "Believe me fella, when I tell ya, he did everything that a man could"-------more words from a song of mine.

Tell Your Children

When I had the chance to see Mao, in Beijing China, I took it. The Chinese kept everyone far away from their dead leader so I couldn't check out if his fingernails were as blue as Lenin's. I learned my lesson in Moscow, Russia.

I was in China for a month which gave me some time to check their dead scene. For adventure, I flew up into central China and floated down the Yangtze River.

The Yangtze River tributaries and their people are undergoing or, should I say, going under water from the completion of the Seven Gorges Dam. These people's dead relatives used to pull all the cargo up that river. They used ropes and walked on the most ingenious mix of bamboo and rope which was lashed to the side of cliffs. Also, in the cliffs, were many caves. These folks buried their dead in the caves. A special group of boys used ropes to lower a man along with fresh dead, Hop Sing and his casket down into a cave. After ten years or so, maybe that same man (if he hadn't fallen to his death) would come down again and tidy up in the cave a bit. If there were older caskets inside, he would check to see how everyone was doing. If Hop Sing was all dried up and nothing but bones, out comes the casket and the bones are placed into an urn. This is very efficient. The only problem I saw for the undertaker was falling to your death every time someone else died.

We floated by village after village as the river rose.

In another village a story was told that the invading army was laughed off the mountain they were on by the king. That had to have been a hell of a laugh.

We visited a site on the top of a cliff. I don't remember the name but I think it was Hell. We walked along a hall and looked at thousands of small statues all carved into terrible depictions of death. There were be-headings, stabbings, and lots of types of deaths being displayed. We were told that that is what Hell is all about.

If you are bad in life, you will live in Hell. In Hell, you will wake up to witness yourself being killed. The pain is real and you get to feel it over and over forever.

And that's just about says it all.

Don't Worry

You've all heard that saying Life's a bitch and then you die.

Before you die you should get out there and do everything you ever wanted to do. If you choose to sit in a chair and watch TV as your life accomplishment, at least get up and move around a bit.

I've pried a couple of your kind free from the chair they had grown into. If you like playing outdoors, get outdoors, I'll get you out from under that tree.

Enjoy life. Death is serious.

Thank you for reading along.

I'll leave you with the words to one of my songs:
        "Tombstone Todd, the Undertaker"
    I'm Tombstone Todd the Undertaker,
    Well, at least that's what I'd done.
    When your days over, don't you worry,
    My day's just begun.
    I'll be your friend, right to the end,
    And a very good friend, indeed.
    Who else do you know who would pick you up?
    When you're dead, and it looks like you peed?
    I'll put you on a table; I'll take off all your clothes.
    Oh my God, the things I've seen
    It's a wonder I didn't turn to stone.
    You ladies have some special tattoos
    In places you wouldn't guess,
    And men, my God, learn to take a bath,
    You really smelled up my place.
    But in the morning, the sun would rise
    And I'd gaze at what I'd done.
    There before me lies a 80 year old man who
    Looks younger than his son.

I'll put you in a shiny box, for all your friends to
see,
Your suit's on right, your hair's combed tight, and
your
Tie's tied perfectly.
My final act of kindness, is a slow cruise through
town
I'll have a toke, fill the caddy up with smoke,
cause
I'm the last to let you down.
I'm Tombstone Todd the Undertaker
Well, at least that's what I'd done.
When your day's over, don't you worry,
My day's just begun.

Remember it's not an undertaking, until the undertaker
undertakes to undertake it.

THE END

www.ingramcontent.com/pod-product-compliance
Lightning Source LLC
Chambersburg PA
CBHW070633290526
45790CB00001B/84

* 9 7 8 1 4 8 4 1 0 0 3 5 6 *